The Art of Self-Awareness:

How to Dig Deep, Introspect, Discover Your Blind Spots, and Truly Know Thyself

By Patrick King
Social Interaction and
Conversation Coach at
www.PatrickKingConsulting
.com

Table of Contents

Introduction

One of the famous Delphic maxims inscribed at the Apollo Temple in Delphi is: Know Thyself. This is precisely what this book is about. But throughout the chapters that follow, we'll see that knowing oneself and knowing *others* are two skills that cannot be developed in isolation. We start by gaining insight into our own thoughts, emotions, and beliefs, and how they inform our behavior. Only when we can understand ourselves in this way, can we understand others. And if we have empathy and compassion towards ourselves, can we practice it for others.

Thus this book is about two skills that act in tandem – self-awareness and social awareness. These two pillars form the foundation of emotional intelligence, and from them, we can construct a way of being that is proven to be more balanced, more robust, more creative, more cooperative and more innovative.

Let's begin with a question: are you self-aware? It's a tricky one, since the quality you are asking about is the same quality you need to answer the question.

Just as most people believe themselves to be above-average drivers (a statistical impossibility) many of us believe we're self-aware, but with little evidence. The ability to correctly assess this quality is itself a component of self-awareness. Just like driving, however, self-awareness is a skill that can be developed... just as much as it can be interfered with and compromised.

The ability to *clearly see and be aware of yourself* has many proven benefits: more confidence and creativity, better decision-making, improved communication skills and more effective leadership strategies, to name a few. And yet there is a major gap between what psychologists and researchers know about the topic, and what is known about deliberately improving this skill out in the real world.

Psychologist Tasha Eurich and colleagues conducted a massive study on self-awareness and gained interesting insights into what it is, what it isn't, and how we can become better at it. Their biggest finding? True self-awareness is rare, with only around 15% of people making the grade. Another big contribution of the study is the discovery there are actually two kinds of self-awareness.

Let's pause and consider that a fixed definition of self-awareness is scarce. The term might refer to the ability to monitor one's own inner experience, or what's broadly called self-consciousness. Or it could be about self-knowledge. But what's going on when someone has a pronounced sense of who they are as a person – that everyone around them disagrees with? Eurich et. al. found there is a difference between *internal* and *external* self-awareness.

Internal: The clarity with which we perceive our innermost desires, emotions, thoughts, values, strengths and weaknesses (i.e. how well you see yourself).
External: The understanding of how other people view us, and the effect we have on

them (i.e. how well you see how others see you).

Those with high internal self-awareness fare better in their jobs, relationships and overall emotional regulation. Those with high external self-awareness are better at empathy and taking on others' perspectives. Both types are positively correlated with overall life success and satisfaction.

What may surprise you is that scoring well in one area doesn't mean you score well in the other. This revelation allowed Eurich to postulate four main self-awareness archetypes, according to where they fall on these two scales.

Low internal SA, low external SA – SEEKERS
Understandably, they don't know who they are or how they appear to others. They may feel aimless, confused, or frustrated in their work and relationships, and be unclear on their own values.

Low internal SA, high external SA – PLEASERS
The tendency is to focus on how they appear to others at the expense of understanding

their perceptions and preferences. They may be well-liked but make decisions often not in their own best interest.

High internal SA, low external SA – INTROSPECTORS

While crystal-clear on their own values and perspectives, they lack insight into how this might differ from other people's experiences of them, which can cause friction or misunderstanding.

High internal SA, High external SA - AWARE

They know who they are and what they want, but also know other people's feedback and opinions, and consider both.

According to Eurich, both types of self-awareness are important, and the most successful individuals are those that have cultivated both capacities simultaneously. If you can correctly identify your type, then you know exactly what to work on when becoming a more rounded and generally self-aware person.

Much self-help literature encourages almost endless development of internal awareness, but unless you also balance that against the perspectives and needs of everyone around you, your awareness will never quite be complete.

Eurich and her team also explored the things that most commonly impede self-awareness, and they honed in on two aspects: **experience** and **power**. Experience can either give us false confidence in our abilities or make us wrongly doubt ourselves – both inhibit accurate self-awareness. For example, the so-called paradox of expertise is where leaders actually become less accurate at assessing their own competence the more experienced they are, while an inexperienced person may underestimate their valuable contribution. Similarly, having a high degree of power makes most people overestimate their self-awareness, competence and empathy (that would explain a lot about our world, wouldn't it?).

Any time you are limiting opportunities for feedback and genuine listening, you risk losing perspective and distorting your own self-awareness. But any time you enlist the insight that comes with constructive feedback, you strengthen self-awareness.

Most interesting of all, the research team found that introspection doesn't lead to better self-awareness. Deeply examining your own thoughts and feelings is valuable, but it turns out it doesn't always help us know ourselves better. Surprisingly, practiced introspectors were *less* self-aware than others. The reason is perhaps obvious: it's so easy to do introspection wrong!

None of us can learn of our unconscious thoughts, and may merely invent explanations and narratives that *feel true*, while giving ourselves no chance to check their accuracy. We may let irrational biases, assumptions and blind spots take over, or get carried away with negative interpretations that muddy the waters.

There is a big, big difference between a clear and rational evaluation of a situation and a completely internal "gut feel" judgment that is plain wrong. Digging deeper and deeper into unfounded hunches and biased beliefs will never genuinely advance your insight, just as mindlessly following other people's interpretations will not give you access to your own.

Again, it's a question of needing *both* types of self-awareness. There is no single "truth," inward or outward, but balancing and awareness of multiple perspectives that allow us real, deep understanding of our lives. Remembering that only 15% of people are *actually* self-aware, the next question should be obvious: how do we get better?

Chapter 1: The three levels of self-awareness

First things first: self-awareness isn't like a single moment of enlightenment, or an off/on switch. It's a matter of degree (or type, as we saw above) and we can be self-aware at some times, less so at others.

We can define self-awareness as **a conscious perception of thoughts, feelings, events and behaviors, both internal and external, that is accurately grounded in reality.**

The opposite of that is anytime we're unconscious (i.e. acting out of habit, impulse or autopilot) or not thinking about how we're thinking. When driven by unconscious impulses and biases, we cannot recognize patterns in our world, and hence we can't take proactive steps to change anything. So many other positive characteristics and

15

traits are impossible without the bedrock of self-awareness, and yet there is little out there that teaches us how to build it within ourselves. And why would we, when most of us think we are self-aware already, right?

With self-awareness comes:
- Self esteem
- Sound decision making
- Creativity
- Self control and emotional regulation
- The ability to develop and evolve
- Humility and awareness of weaknesses
- Pride
- Empathy
- Communication and cooperation

However, reading the above list, you can probably see that it's all shades of grey. To simplify, we can imagine there are 3 levels of self awareness we can operate from:

Level 1: What are you doing?

Pain, confusion, suffering, stress, irritation, misunderstanding, struggle etc. life is This is like at low levels of self-awareness. If you're unhappy with work, relationships, money or life, you probably have some self-awareness blindspots. In this mind space, we are unhappy yet unaware of the reasons *why*, unaware of our role in the problem, and oblivious about what we can do to fix it.

Signs you're in this level include any behavior that transports you out of the present moment. This could include numbing yourself out with distractions and addictions such as gaming, mindless social media use, substance abuse, or bingeing – whether on food or media. We avoid obligations and feel so anxious, angry or apathetic that we procrastinate. Worse still, we aren't even aware that we're doing all this.

For example, you have an awkward discussion with a family member and find yourself overeating that evening and feeling too lazy to do any chores. Then you go to bed late after a four-hour gaming binge and wake up the next morning with a sour mood and a sore head. But you don't understand *why* any of this is happening. You are unaware of how you feel after the conversation, you are unaware that bingeing and gaming were your coping mechanisms, and you're unaware that the reason you feel so bad the next morning is because of these choices.

So you have a vague, dull sense of "my life sucks" and you march onwards, oblivious, and unable to help yourself. How could you, when you are unaware of the nature and existence of the problem? Distraction is destructive. But infinitely more destructive is any compulsive behavior *that we are not aware of*. Without awareness, we are slaves at the mercy of... well, everything. We forfeit our free will.

Don't try to vanquish distraction – the harder and more pressing task is to just learn you are distracted! How often have you fallen down an internet rabbit hole, when you don't even remember what brought you to your phone or laptop in the first place?

This is the frustrating paradox of self-awareness: we *think* we are so much better at it than we are. To prove this point, try a simple exercise: simply become aware of how much time you're spending on distractions. Changing behavior comes later – first, we just want to learn of the extent of addictive, compulsive behavior. Many people deliberately waste time or indulge in a little distraction, but they do it with full conscious awareness. Different story. Likewise, if you're completely mindless during a meditation session, it's as useless as if you were gaming or stuffing your face or losing hours on a Netflix binge. The behvaior is only a symptom; the real issue is awareness.

If you are at level 1 (most of us are at some point) then try to objectively track and monitor your distraction behaviors for a fixed period, such as a week. You can use an app to track your social media or gaming use, or you could commit to jotting down precisely what you eat and when every day. At this point, you are not judging these observations. You are just becoming curious about what is happening, and to what extent.

Level 2: What are you feeling?

When you become aware of and gradually start to remove distractions, you will be confronted with all the emotions those distractions covered up. What you've been avoiding will come rushing out in full force. If you're the kind to get freaked out by silence or having nothing to do, this will likely be why! When we have unprocessed, unacknowledged emotions (i.e. emotions we're not fully aware of) it hurts. We would do anything to patch over them with more lovely, safe distractions.

This second level of self-awareness comes from understanding not just what we are doing (scoffing tubs of ice cream) but why we are doing it, and how it feels (you're stressed and angry, and need the comfort of something sweet). When you are in touch with what you actually, genuinely feel, and are no longer distracted and numbed out by the carousel of everyday distractions, you start to have original thoughts, and become aware of feelings you never even knew you had.

For example, a woman spends 20 years of her life married to a man, but one day thinks, "oh my God, how did I end up here? I have nothing in common with this person." Throughout her marriage there was some comfortable distraction: raising the kids, keeping up with work, moving house, dealing with family crises... but when the couple retire together, there is for the first time in years a quiet moment where the ordinary distractions are absent. The feelings that have always been there are more clearly revealed. The *doing* has concealed the *feeling*. Had she asked "what am I doing?" and answered honestly, she might have answered, "avoiding facing the truth" and simultaneously discovered what she was feeling. This is the way that level 1 awareness can inspire level 2 awareness.

Maintaining awareness can be difficult because facing certain emotions is uncomfortable. It hurts! We don't *want* to know how afraid we are, or angry, or weak. Many people spend their entire lives having literally no idea how they feel. Instead, they mimic others or repeat stories about what they think they feel, and anytime they get even slightly close to being aware of deep, genuine feelings, they abruptly switch off and engage in distraction and addiction instead. After all, being aware of difficult feelings usually means we have to take some action – leave a partner, quit a job, do better, make an effort. And that can be scary.

At this level, there is one powerful but tricky lesson to master, and that is that emotions are just... emotions. They are always there, flowing like the sea, but they don't necessarily *mean* anything, and they are not the be-all and end-all. When you are conscious and accepting of them, you discover something important: they flow on. You don't have to chase "good" emotions or run screaming from "bad" ones. Feeling a lot isn't necessarily profound. In fact, emotions in themselves can be distractions... from other emotions!

Again we arrive at what's important: not the emotions themselves, but the awareness behind them. Don't become that person hooked on an "enlightenment" loop. You need not get lost in endless self-reflection (like the "introspector" described above). Remember, navel-gazing is *not* the same as self-awareness. The *feeling* of profundity and awareness is not the same as actual awareness (don't analyze that too closely!). You could get addicted to the process of endlessly digging through layer upon layer since you will always find something that feels pithy.

But is it? Does it illuminate, clarify and show you what's what? Usually no.

Digging down to ever-deeper layers is a trap because it only *feels* important. Practically speaking, it creates anxiety rather than self-awareness and genuine insight. We'll look at anxiety more in later chapters, but although emotions are valid, they are not a substitution for self-awareness. Emotions can help or hinder. They can be appropriate or inappropriate, helpful or unhelpful. But they all pass. And we can strengthen our ability to "sit with" our emotions, without clinging or judgment, and fully know what they are while still not allowing them to push us around.

Level 3: What are you not aware of?

You can become aware of what you're doing, i.e. your behavior. You can become aware of the associated thoughts, emotions and beliefs around that. But the final level of self-awareness is bringing into your conscious mind all those things that you are *not* aware of. If you are diligently focusing on your actions, thoughts and feelings, you'll soon notice something: how much nonsense there is. Really.

You may have a bunch of ill-conceived and rather stupid ideas, kneejerk reactions, habitual behaviors that don't make sense, automatic responses you just inherited from someone else, big heaping doses of arrogance and ego, fear, stubborn opposition and resistance, lazy thinking, and ideas you cling to desperately despite them being irrational and outdated. Oh, and on top of all of this, you probably still hold tightly onto the idea that you are an impressive independent thinker, ultra-smart, kind, funny, and generally one of the good guys. Right?

Here lies one of the first big obstacles to genuine self-awareness: we're stubborn idiots who believe we already are self-aware! Yet the research consistently shows that our memories are unreliable, that we overestimate our abilities, that our focus is often distorted and self-serving, that we lie a little to make ourselves feel better, and that we're not all that good at assessing risk, making statistical judgments or genuinely taking on board constructive criticism.

Phew! Here's the thing, though: none of this is a problem, so long as we are aware of it. This is an issue only if we are plowing ahead with it, unaware. We all have weaknesses. The true test is not to be faultless, but to bravely and honestly accept the faults you have, and take reasonable action to work around them.

Many of us unconsciously believe that a heightened state of self-awareness is simply everything we hold in our minds, only somehow amplified. In fact, the process of developing increased self-awareness is often felt to be a *diminishing* project, because we lose precious illusions, patterns, fantasies, unrealistic expectations and all those problems we were creating for ourselves. It's taking ourselves less seriously, getting real, and admitting that we know a loss less than we thought we did.

Imagine a guy who prides himself on being a deep thinking academic type. Immediately after finishing his first degree, he dives into another, despite not being able to afford it, and despite it being unnecessary for his intended career. He spends a lot of time fretting over getting it all done, and makes a martyr of himself, secretly relishing how impressed everyone sounds when they hear he is tackling yet another degree. He fills his days with a busy schedule of what he believes is enriching self-development. He even feels a little superior to those who haven't acquired his academic achievements. All the while, he is an intelligent individual dutifully going to therapy each week, where he uses big words to talk about everything from his minor family dramas to his girlfriend.

Looks pretty good. But what is he not aware of?

If he were honest and had genuine self-awareness, he would see that his insistence on being a lifelong student is a way to cope with the fear of actually going out into the world to get a "real job." Rather than tackle his blind spots and weaknesses head-on, he plays at tackling others that feel easier to manage. Nobody can say he isn't working on himself if he's feverishly pursuing his education, right? He has concealed the real reason for his actions even from himself. His careful avoidance of having to face his fears of inadequacy and failure means he never mentions it to his therapist, and she never asks. So long as there is a mountain of coursework for him to get through, he spares himself the awareness of what has been forcefully shoved aside: the immobilizing terror he has at the prospect of having to work.

One important thing to realize is that we can only be better with empathy and understanding other people's emotions and thoughts, once we are operating at *all three* of these levels ourselves. If you are a person religiously avoiding your emotions in your own life, all you could do when confronted with someone else's strong emotion is to avoid it in much the same way. If you're the person whose coping strategy is to numb out pain with distractions, then what insight could you generate into the causes of someone else's life troubles? This is perhaps what people mean when they say that your relationship with others reflects the relationship with yourself. The guy in our example above may never encounter his unconscious drives, but he will see hints of it: in his disproportionate judgment of "losers" and in his inability to tolerate fear and self-doubt when he finds it in others.

To support our goal of cultivating greater total self-awareness, internal and external, we have many tools at our disposal. We can commit to holding weaker opinions, taking ourselves less seriously, and being honest about our blind spots and ingrained patterns. We can learn to anchor in reality and actively seek the feedback and perspectives of others, and have the courage the face our weaknesses and actively change them.

Kegan's theory of adult development

Let's consider a model that can help us pull together some of these ideas around awareness, which as we've seen, is not so much a fixed trait but a skill that can be refined and practiced over time. The fact is, self-awareness is a capacity that grows with us. Our perception of self and others, and how well we know the rules for engaging with them, start evolving from the moment we're born. While most people understand that children develop according to milestones, they might not be aware that adults do, too. In fact, according to psychologist Robert Kegan, adults mature along a course of 5 developmental stages.

And what makes a mature adult? It's the ability to gain both awareness of the inner self and grow in social maturity, responsibility, independent thought, self-control and wisdom. Kegan's research estimated that a full 65% of people do not make it past stage 3 of 5, meaning they do not become "high functioning" with social behavior, relationships and work.

The key is, surprise surprise, awareness. So let's begin with the obvious: we need to know what the stages are, and where we fall. This gives us something to aim for, and helps us think clearly about the capacities we're still developing. But before we race ahead with the stages (admit it – you're dying to know how you score, right?) let's clarify two important related concepts that underpin the overall theory.

The first is **transformation**. Consider a caterpillar. To develop, it's not enough to simply be a better and better caterpillar. Instead, a complete shift is required, i.e. it needs to become a whole new being: a butterfly. With humans, it's the same. The developmental path is not to simply learn new things and refine existing skills – it's to completely change the *way* you perceive and engage with the world. The former is about changing what you put in the container, the latter is about completely changing the container itself. We are not merely growing, but *transforming*.

The second is the **subject-object shift**. Kegan believed that as we develop and mature as adults, we necessarily undergo a shift from knowing the world as a subject (that is, something that controls us) to knowing it as an object (something that we can control). In the first mode, we are bound up and tangled in self-concepts and unable to reflect on them – we feel like *are* them. In the second, we can detach from these self-concepts and consider them as something separate from ourselves. As we do, we realize our agency and ability to change, control or reinterpret these concepts. We become more "objective," more proactive, and we develop this all-important capacity for self-awareness.

Subject – "I **am**" i.e. total identification, the concept controls you (example, "I *am* a father, it's just who I am")
Object – "I **have**" i.e. can perceive from a distance, you control the concept (example, "the fatherhood role is something I *have*, it's something I can choose to do. I can step back from the idea and make conscious choices about what being a father means.")

A further example will clarify. When we're younger, we may automatically identify with our parent's political beliefs, and say something like, "I'm a liberal" without thinking too deeply about it. We are in subject mode, and take this perspective as a given, and something that determines us, rather than something that we determine.

Later, as we grow up, we see ourselves as independent agents, i.e. people who *have* beliefs – and if you take on a belief, it also means you can drop it, too.

You may have an epiphany in early adulthood where you realize that you are actually in control of what you believe. Stepping back, you can reflect on the issues independently, and make a choice about your perspectives and beliefs, and consequently how you will act. This is a drastic transformation. Before, you might have automatically behaved in the way that you thought "liberals" behaved, i.e. you lacked self-awareness. But now, the concept of "liberal" is something you are free to choose, or not. Being aware, you may well choose the same thing again, but it is now from a completely different and more mature perspective. From the objective perspective, your feelings and thoughts are not who you **are**, they are something you **have**. If you are aware of this fact, then you can *choose*. As our awareness and consciousness evolve, we advance in maturity.

Most of us are somewhere between stages. Each stage is characterized by what is achieved as an object, i.e. what area of life we can transform and experience a subject-object shift in. Few go beyond stage 3.

Stage 1 and 2: The Early Stages
From early childhood to adolescence (or, to be frank, adulthood for some)

We'll consider the early two stages only briefly, as they largely correspond to childhood development. The earliest stage is called **incorporative**, and there is little sense of self to speak of, i.e. no distinction between self and other. Infants and babies are more or less enmeshed in their sensory experience, and their task is the transformative understanding there are things out in the world that are *not* self. So, in Kegan's terms, the child learns to think, "my reflexes and sensory awareness are not me, they are something that I have."

From around 6 years onwards to adolescence is stage 2, called the **impulsive** stage (exact terminology varies). Here, the self is learning about impulses but is still very identified with them. Whilst babies have no understanding of anything objective at all, and inhabit only their own perspective, in the second stage there is a growing awareness of others as independent beings. However, these beings, for example, parents, are still perceived concerning the self's own impulses, and in terms of how they satisfy those impulses or not.

If you are at stage 1 or 2, the emphasis will be exclusively on your own needs, perspectives impulses, agendas and desires. In so far as you can appreciate other people, your engagement with them is transactional, i.e. to meet your desires and needs.

*Subject: the self **IS** one's needs, interests & desires*
*Object: the self **HAS** impulses, perceptions & emotions*

Such a person may act morally and consider the needs of others, but it's always ultimately to serve their own needs, for example, kindness is given expecting it will accrue benefits for the self later on.

People in these early levels are low in internal and external self-awareness, and they align with ideologies, philosophies, perspectives and rules, not from genuine belief, but from a feeling there is some reward or punishment associated with doing so. For example, if you asked someone in this stage why stealing was wrong, their reply might talk about the legal consequences or punishments from others (subject mode) rather than the innate ethics or the appeal to personal values (object mode).

Stage 3: The socialized mind

From adolescence onwards

*Subject: **IS** interpersonal relationships*
*Object: **HAS** needs, interests & desires*

According to Kegan, most of us stop developing at around this stage. We can consider that it's here that our external self-awareness develops – i.e. where the outside world shapes our perception of both self and reality.

The focus at this stage is on ideas, beliefs, conventions and norms as they are presented by the social systems around us. So, we look externally to our families, our societies, our histories and our cultures to determine who we are and what we believe. We experience ourselves as others experience us, substituting their view for our internal experience. For example, if those around us tell us "You're worthless" then we don't say, "They think I'm worthless" but rather "I am worthless."

We may spend a lot of time managing and taking responsibility for other people's experiences, and require external validation to feel any sense of value in ourselves. This is the phenomenon of not knowing how to rate or appraise something until we're sure how others will rate it. In a deep sense, we are unsure of whether we are good or bad until someone or something tells us we are.

We may appear to have high external self-awareness, but we lack an independent sense of self (internal self-awareness) and struggle to understand what we value, what we want, or who we are, outside of other people's perspectives. To reach this stage, we now no longer view relationships as transactional, and we know that other people possess their own perspectives. However, the interpersonal relationship is the focus and we can care so much about what others think that we internalize their perspectives.

If you ask a person in this stage why stealing is wrong, they may answer in terms of values and belief systems, or the effects on important social relationships. However, these values and beliefs depend on external rules and ideologies. The socialized mind says something like "I **am** my relationships. I follow the rules." Note how this is the subject speaking.

Stage 4: The self-authoring mind

*Subject: **IS** self-authorship, identity and ideology*
*Object: **HAS** relationships*

Kegan found that whereas around 65% of adults inhabit the previous stage, just 35% fall into this level. Here, a person may still not detach from their identities and personal ideologies, even though they have made the realization they are not their relationships, but rather they *have* relationships. This is the level where we are no longer defined by others, by our society, by our relationships, or by our engagement with the environment. Instead, we self-determine. The big understanding is that we are autonomous humans with feelings and thoughts independent of others, and the environment.

At this stage, we may be heavily focused on the person we are, as exemplified by our values, desires and limitations. We know how to stand up for what we believe in, and our ability to think independently gives us our unique voice. Because we take responsibility for our own state of mind, we have a more nuanced, contextual understanding of the world and ourselves in it. We've had the experience of ourselves as purpose-driven and value-oriented, and we understand that we can change these things about ourselves.

Ask such a person to explain why stealing is wrong and they will give you a highly original, carefully considered response that centers them as authoritative, moral beings who can choose their values and their aligning actions. They may something like, "others can steal if they want, but humans have free will, and I choose to be a person of integrity. I'm a good person, and I know, in my heart, what is right. Character comes from our choices, and my inner compass tells me the right choice."

Stage 5: The interconnected mind

*Subject: **IS***
*Object: **HAS** self-authorship,   identity   and ideology*

Kegan claimed that just 1% of people ever reached this stage. Here, the person's sense of self is not attached to *any* identities or roles. Instead, there is only endless exploration of potential identities, roles, perspectives and engagements with others. The self is dynamic and ever-flowing, and we can spontaneously and repeatedly find balance in every emerging moment. We consider both our inner experience and the feedback from others. We can appreciate and "hold" complexity without needing to collapse everything into a concrete, fixed set of concepts that we are then held prisoner to.

We are expansive and unlimited. As our circumstances change, we change too. We are able to do something that is only associated with this stage: contain paradox. We are not only comfortable genuinely considering perspectives outside of our own, but we can also inhabit them and apparently opposed viewpoints *simultaneously*. We can "contain multitudes."

Ask a person in this level about the morality of stealing, and they will be able to question the very frame of reference that makes such a query possible. They will easily entertain the full arena of possible perspectives on the question, perhaps even generating novel and original models or theories about the concept of morality itself ("who is this Kegan guy anyway, and wouldn't I like to make my own model instead?"). They will become interested not just in the different ideas, but in what connects them, what lies underneath and beyond them, and the meta-perspective that allows contradictions to dissolve.

They won't cling too hard to any of these ideas, however, and will not wear any pet theory as a cloak of identity – in fact, you can expect them to handle their contemplations with humor and irreverence. They can seamlessly and without ego set down one set of assumptions and genuinely consider another set, zooming in and out and ultimately abandoning assumptions completely.

They are comfortable with not making definitive pronouncements. They understand that intellectual faculties can be utilitarian, i.e. something that you have and use, rather than something that you are. One way of knowing and thinking will work at one time and in one context, but not in another. Their skill lies not in the content of their thoughts or the quality of their connection to others, but in the fluency with which they can adopt both.

So, which stage are you currently in?

Kegan found something similar to Eurich and colleagues in that most people overestimate their maturity and awareness. You may have resonated with some descriptions above, but remember that we can straddle stages, occupy certain stages intermittently, or confuse being at a certain level with *wanting* to be there.

To be on the safe side, assume that you are one level below where you think you are. According to Kegan's theory:

- We advance to higher levels when we make **transformations** to our style of knowledge and engagement (both of which require awareness)
- We transform when what was once viewed as subject is viewed as object, i.e. we make a **subject-object shift**

- **What is acquired and mastered in one level is the challenge for the preceding level**. Thus, to advance, we need to make the appropriate transformation and shift what we currently hold as a subject into an object.

This sounds more complicated than it is. No matter which level we're at, our developmental goal is always to change our subjective experience of the world into objective, i.e. place more and more of our self-concept under our own control. Let's look at the example of religious views.

Stage 1: You don't even have a self, you are merely a collection of sensory perceptions, and the overarching need to be loved and cared for. You ARE those needs.

Stage 2: You soon realize that you are a separate being from your parents, and that you as a being have needs, rather than being identified with those needs. As a young teenager, you can see that your parents are independent of you, but you consider them only in terms of how well they provide you with the love you need.

Stage 3: Once you can see you are a separate being that *has* needs, your focus shifts to your all-important relationship with your parents. You identify as their child. You are identified with the attunement, relationship and connection you experience with them. They are Christians; this means you are too. As you grow into young adulthood, your culture, educational environment and friendship circles are Christian, and, since you value them and your relationship with them, you concur and are a Christian too.

Stage 4: You realize these relationships, though important, are not the essence of who you are. With identity and ideology, you feel that you are a self-determining being who isn't defined by relationships but merely has them. You instead define yourself on your terms – you may wonder deeply about the Christian faith and grow attached to other self-concepts. Maybe you run away to the mountains to become a Buddhist, and you focus intently for years on your ability to author your own experience.

Stage 5: You run out of money and come back home. You haven't found enlightenment, but have a deeper realization: that your Buddhist identity was also just something you *had*, and not something you *were*. You are happy just to be, and keep your identity fluid and responsive. You return to Christianity and see it with completely new eyes. One day, while you're out walking, you have an epiphany and realize that, from a certain perspective, you have been a Christian all along... as well as Buddhist... and Jewish too... plus a complete atheist...

Kegan saw maturity as a function of expanding objectivity, and for him, being objective was a question of distance instead of identification. That distance is the same thing as self-awareness. In the chapters that follow, we will essentially look at practical ways to develop objectivity in ourselves and gain self-awareness as we do so.

Summary:

- There are two types of self-awareness: *internal* (how aware we are of our thoughts, feelings and identities) and *external* (how aware we are of how we are perceived by others). Internal awareness doesn't always imply external awareness. We can be seekers (low on both types), introspectors (high only on internal SA), people-pleasers (high only on external SA) or fully aware (high on both).

43

- Self-awareness develops as a capacity throughout life, and progresses through stages. Level 1 concerns the awareness of what you are doing and the causes of behavior. Level 2 is about awareness of what you are feeling, which is often concealed by what you are doing. Level 3 is awareness not only of thoughts, feelings and actions, but of what is being pushed out of awareness or avoided. This is the stage of deeper insight into the self.
- Kegan's theory of adult development showed that self-awareness matures with age, with people gradually acquiring more objectivity. We can progress through stages, where we **transform** (that is, change the way we perceive, rather than the content of what we perceive) and make **subject-object shifts**.
- We mature when we transform from subjective experience to objective. This can be simplified as the ability to see you "**have**" a quality that you can step back from and observe, rather than you "**are**" a quality that you are completely identified with.
- We can see increasing self-awareness as a project of gaining more objectivity in place of subjective identification.

Chapter 2: Reassessing beliefs from your past, and your dark side

Subject: This is the way things are.
Object: *Why* are they this way? And could they be some other way? What can I do to change things? What do I want?

In Kegan's stages 4 and 5, we begin to question ourselves, our beliefs, and the source of those beliefs, rather than taking them as given. In Kegan's framework, mature development into adulthood is about learning to stand on your own two feet, ideologically speaking.

Thus, you move from being a conventional, rule-bound and socialized member of a group, to an independent, autonomous agent who generates their values and beliefs. In this model, certain beliefs and ideologies come from externally, for example from culture. But on the path to gaining greater self-awareness, we also need to pay heed to those beliefs that stem from within us.

Understanding the shadow

According to Carl Jung, every human comprises both dark and light, good and bad. But we can hold some parts of our identities in awareness, and push unwanted or disowned parts into the unconscious mind, or what he called "the shadow."

Here, light is a metaphor for conscious awareness, and not a moral judgment – we may, for example, also push away from our awareness the knowledge of objectively "good" traits. A little girl may push into the shadow her larger-than-life personality, her ebullience and strength, and her ambition, because her family tell her it's not lady-like. A little boy may push from his awareness his own enormous empathy and gentleness, because his society sends him constant messages that the traits are for women only.

Every human is whole and complete, but when we exist in families, cultures and societal ideologies, some of what we are is labelled bad, and some is labelled good. We fracture into parts. As infants, we depend on our parents for survival – their approval and validation of us is a matter of life or death! – so we adapt accordingly. We learn to suppress what is unwanted and bring to light what is valued by others.

As a child you may have shown aggression and anger to a sibling, only to be harshly reprimanded by your parents. You learn that the aggressive and angry part of you is not welcome, so you push it out of conscious awareness. You grow into a kind, calm and non-aggressive adult horrified at the suggestion that you are in any way aggressive.

But, the aggression is still there. It has only been pushed deep down into the unconscious mind. This aggression may peep out in dreams, or show its head in unexpected places. And while it's there, it may continue to affect your decision-making, your actions, your thoughts and feelings – all unconsciously.

As you can see, the deciding factor is again awareness.

Jung once said, "Until you make the unconscious conscious, it will direct your life and you will call it fate." In other words, if something is in our shadow, it will always control us and we will always be at its mercy because we are unaware of it. But if we can learn of who we are – *all* of who we are – then we are empowered to change it.

Thus, the person who has low internal and external self-awareness may feel endlessly plagued by personal demons they can't control and don't understand. But when they get a grasp on themselves and shine the light of awareness onto their *full* experience, they can take charge and proactively make decisions. This is precisely the difference between subject and object that Kegan described.

When we disown certain parts of ourselves, we divide and become fractured. We may feel like strangers to ourselves. Our shadow could be completely steering our entire life, without us ever knowing it. And each time we allow the shadow to control us unconsciously, it grows stronger.

The trick is: how do you know what you don't know? Or, returning to a question we had in a previous chapter, how can you become aware of what you're not aware of?

For Jung, there were always clues that the mind was hiding things from itself. Have you ever done something and not understood why you did it? Have you ever felt yourself slipping into an old pattern and habit, almost as though in a dream, powerless to stop or do anything else? Have you ever felt yourself having an extreme and seemingly disproportionate reaction to something? Your shadow is likely at work in all three cases.

Returning to awareness, your shadow may also be at work when you constantly feel unsure of who you are (because a big part of who you are is outside your awareness), at odds with other people's perceptions of you (because they can only engage with certain parts of you) and conflicted with the world (because who you are and what you broadcast to others does not align).

Here are two big red flags telling you that your shadow is in play:

You project onto others

For the mind, one of the best ways to disown a part of itself is to throw it away and claim it belongs to someone else! For example, a cheating husband is unwilling to face that he is living a dishonest life, and instead finds himself extra-suspicious of his wife, jealousy accusing her of hiding things. She isn't, of course. *He* is the one hiding things – from himself. What he has done is project his repressed dishonesty onto her. If she carries it, then he can freely condemn it; his lashing out at her is the displaced rejection of his dishonest behavior.

Want to know if you're projecting? Take a hard look at what you judge, condemn and criticize most frequently in others. You know the thing you most strenuously deny you'd never, ever, ever do? Become more curious about *that* thing...

You're triggered
When you're triggered, you're not responding to something in the moment, but to a memory of something traumatic or unwanted in the past – something you might not even consciously remember. For example, you have a complete meltdown one day when a partner disappears and fails to answer their phone for a few hours. Triggers

like this can be thought of as helpful messengers from the dark side, alerting us to all the parts of our psyche not yet integrated. They are like emissaries saying, "this needs more awareness." In this example, you may realize that the triggers point to old, unconscious trauma around being abandoned as a child.

Think of the shadow this way: it *wants* to come out into conscious awareness. It's part of you. And it will keep trying to restore you to wholeness. If you cannot yet allow it into conscious awareness, it will work in strange ways to make itself known anyway.

Now, a word of warning: shadow work is, unsurprisingly, a murky area in the psychological and self-development worlds. Some people feel that it's unnecessary, even dangerous. Others argue that it's precisely because we're so avoidant and fearful that the shadow has a hold on us – and it's only by embracing our total selves we can achieve the wellbeing we want.

Shadow work sounds... well, dark. And a little intimidating. But in truth it is simply growing our awareness, much in the way as in Kegan's theory, we develop as we move from unconscious, passive and subjective to conscious, proactive and objective. This is not threatening or angst-filled; rather, it's a process of "calling home" old parts of yourself that were long cut off. It's a broadening, healing activity that will leave you feeling larger and more completely yourself.

Using awareness to integrate the shadow

Well so much for the theory. How can we use the concept of the shadow to improve our overall self-awareness, in everyday life?

The idea is to **integrate**. You want to look at all those disinherited parts of yourself and say, "Yes, I accept that. That's me!" From Kegan's perspective, integrating the shadow aligns with taking increased material from the subjective realm, and bringing it into the objective realm.

Note that you are not at all trying to be perfect, trying to get rid of your shadow, or trying to BS your way into believing that your weaknesses have actually been amazing strengths all along. You are merely doing something very mature – realizing that you are a complex human with both good and bad sides. And that's perfectly OK.

To be 100% clear: we don't kill the shadow, we integrate it. And integrating it does not mean changing it into something else, but accepting it courageously and honestly for what it is – a part of us.

Here's a simple method for using your own beliefs and assumptions to help you get in touch with your shadow. Usually, our most deeply held assumptions and personal beliefs were programmed in childhood, where our shadow was first created.

Step 1: Become aware of any moment where you feel you have been triggered, confused, or overwhelmed by strong emotions you didn't understand. You may only do a kind of "postmortem" after the fact, but that's OK. It's a good idea to sit with a journal and slowly and carefully work through the following question: <u>when did you first feel this way?</u>

Example: Your boss asked you to deliver a presentation to the team on a topic you're an expert in. You were thrilled! So why did you procrastinate on preparing anything, and cancel at the last minute? You feel awful but don't know why, and you snap defensively at a colleague who asks you a question. You ask

55

yourself – when did you first feel this way? You remember that you were a gregarious and creative child. But you also recall an episode where your mom asked you to show her your ballet moves, and you felt mortified and refused, and felt this same feeling.

Step 2: Look more closely at this first feeling. Thinking back to past experiences, <u>what did you learn then about what was *good* and *bad* about yourself?</u> What were the unspoken "rules" of living in your household? Can you formulate these feelings into a core belief?

Example: Digging into the memory, you discover an even earlier memory where you did share your creative expression with your parents, only to have them laugh at you and dismiss your efforts. You learnt that creative expression was valued, but only if it was perfect – if you goofed around or improvised or got too excited, then this was bad.

You realize that many of your current beliefs have their origin in these early experiences:

"It's embarrassing to make a mistake."
"If you can't do it perfectly, don't even bother."

"Giddy excitement is childish and laughable."

"Creative endeavors are performances for other people, and not done for your own pleasure."

Step 3: <u>Name it and claim it – without judgment or shame</u>. Look at those parts of yourself that you long ago decided were unacceptable, and gently try to pull them back into yourself. It's very important not to judge either the content in your shadow or the reasons you had for suppressing awareness in the first place.

You don't have to love what you find – just accept it and acknowledge its existence. The shadow is born from non-awareness, which itself comes from non-acceptance. We reverse this process when we shine a non-judgmental light on everything we become aware of.

Example: You realize that although your parents thought that your exuberance, energy and creative expression were flawed and inadequate, these things are nevertheless a part of you, and *you* can accept them as such. You consciously choose not to criticize yourself for cutting off this part of you. You feel a little self-compassion for your younger self, who was only doing the best she could at the time.

Step 4: Put your shadow in the passenger seat. Now it's time to see how this past childhood experience has shaped and created your perception today. When you're unconscious of it, it runs your life. When you're conscious, though, you can be aware of it without letting it control you. Ask yourself: <u>how has my shadow, and the beliefs it created, impacted my life?</u> What is their role in the current situation? Finally, explore how you want to behave now, in the moment. <u>Do you want to choose something else?</u>

Example: You come back to the present and realize that when your boss praised your enthusiasm and demanded you perform for the team, this triggered the childhood memory of your parents judging you. A series of core beliefs, thoughts and feelings were set off, and before you knew it you had cancelled the presentation. Now you know why – you feared being judged.

Congratulations! You have now created distance between you and these beliefs that no longer serve you. You can step back and *decide consciously* what you want to do, instead of simply reacting emotionally. You call your boss and apologize, asking if you can do the presentation. It'll be scary, but also healing, because it will allow you to reclaim all those parts of yourself that you had cut off – whether the team likes your presentation or not!

Many people believe the shadow can be thought of as a temporary holding place, or a blind spot where we store those things that we're *not yet* ready to become aware of. However, as we grow and evolve, and as we're ready to integrate, these things will increasingly come to awareness. Let's shift our perspective. Let's look at friction, strong emotions or confusion as an invitation to go deeper into our shadow, and integrate now what we could not back then.

The next time you feel strong emotions or ideas and experiences that don't feel like they belong to you somehow, pay attention and run through the above steps:

- When did you first feel this feeling?
- What were you taught as a child was "good" and "bad" about you?

- How has this shaped your core beliefs?
- Can you name what you see in your shadow without judgment?
- From the present moment, and inspired by your own values, how would you like to change that core belief?

Getting acquainted with your core beliefs

When we become aware of the self, exactly what are we becoming aware of anyway?

Some would say it's our core beliefs. Whether you call it an attitude, mindset, perspective, set of values, preferences or priorities, your unique collection of core beliefs functions like a prime directive or program that guides and shapes everything in your life. It's not quite *who you are*, but rather the internal rules you follow that help you understand yourself and the world around you.

Your personality, identity and sense of history are made up of stories, and these stories are colored and interpreted according to your core beliefs. The function of these beliefs is to organize and shape your experiences into a coherent whole that makes sense to you. If your parents repeatedly behaved as though you were extremely special and lovable, then you may naturally develop a core belief of "well, I guess I *am* special and lovable." If bad things kept happening to you for no reason, your mind would try to make sense of it and come up with a helpful heuristic: "life isn't fair, and you cannot expect to ever get what you want."

And just as Kegan described above, when we are immature and first being taught about the world, we internalize and identify strongly with our core beliefs. We are in the subjective mode, in other words, and we take our beliefs about ourselves and the world as 100% gospel. It doesn't even look like a core belief to us, it just looks like… reality. Like our shadow, it controls and drives everything, and yet we are completely oblivious to its existence.

So, although core beliefs are there for a reason, and though they were the best our immature and developing minds could do at the time, they are not always accurate, healthy or helpful. To develop, you guessed it: we need to go into objective mode, to see our beliefs *as beliefs*, and to find the transformative maturity that comes with changing them. We need awareness.

And there is very good reason to change core beliefs that are no longer working. Our core beliefs are not just flimsy opinions that float around on the surface of our being – they go deep, and they affect every aspect of our lives. Our core beliefs, in the biggest way possible, determine our experience. They not only influence how we interpret events and what we choose to focus on, they determine the actions we take, which of course can send us down certain paths in life, close us off to particular opportunities or create feedback with the environment that then affirms or amplifies those choices.

Our beliefs influence our thoughts and feelings, and these in turn create our focus, our priorities and most importantly, our actions. This becomes our character, and our character manifests as events, relationships and situations "out there" in the world. The most effective way to significantly change your life is, ironically, not to change your life at all, but to change the core beliefs that influence your perception of that life.

How you think, feel and believe is a stimulus on reality – think of your attitude as a force field around you that elicits certain reactions from others. You can create self-fulfilling prophesies – for example, if you believe "I am lovable" then you will broadcast that clearly, tending to attract other people who agree and treat you with kindness and respect.

Look at your life as it is and imagine that it is a material expression of not only objective reality, but your unique relationship to it – a relationship mediated by your beliefs about that reality. Change the beliefs, and everything else changes, too. Again, we are talking about the conceptual leaps, and the deep transformations that take us from one way of seeing into another. Until we change the beliefs programming our current life, we make no meaningful or sustainable change.

And this is where awareness comes in. If we are aware of our core beliefs, we can change them. If we aren't, we will simply continue acting from within that paradigm. Like Einstein famously said, we cannot solve a problem at the same level of thinking that created that problem in the first place. We need to look beyond and take as an object our own way of thinking, and our assumptions.

Adopting new, healthier beliefs that more accurately align with reality and which serve us well is difficult. But it's much easier than the alternative! With self-awareness, beliefs go from being torturers and controllers, to being useful and exciting tools that can help us achieve what's important to us. *We* use *them*, and not the other way round. If something doesn't work? We can change it to something that does.

What is the life your core beliefs create for you?

Most of us think we're perceiving reality pretty neutrally, but that's because our most stubborn prejudices, beliefs and assumptions are so ingrained that they're invisible to us. We're like the person who thinks that they don't have an accent, but everyone else does. The easiest way to become aware of the program you're running, so to speak, is to observe the outputs. Look at the way you speak, behave, and relate. Look at what you create, what you focus on, and what you ignore. Your core beliefs (even those that you've shoved away into the shadow) are out in plain sight if you only look:

Consider what you're projecting onto others
As we saw earlier, the things that irritate you most about others are often a reflection of something you are less accepting of and less aware of in yourself. Remember, even though we may be unaware of what our core beliefs are, we are still run by them, and still act according to their vision of reality.

So, notice how you treat others, especially those that you dislike, fear or are confused by. If you notice a strong negative reaction to someone else, ask yourself, *what core belief is at the root of this reaction?* Core beliefs can be layered – dig deeper and you will find even more fundamental ones waiting underneath.

For example, you find yourself feeling judgmental of someone who earns less than you. What does this reflect about you and your beliefs about yourself, money, and human value? You may find that the core belief driving your initial judgment of them is the same one you apply to yourself: "income is the only measure of a person's worth." How is this core belief playing out in your world?

Be mindful
This may seem obvious, but one way to foster more awareness in yourself is to... practice. Practice being aware, in the moment, right now. Meditation and mindfulness are simply ways to strengthen the muscle of conscious awareness. Remembering that aimless contemplation and introspection is not associated with greater self-awareness, use meditation for what it has been proven effective for: emotional regulation.

Doing a simple breath-focused meditation every day can teach you to go into object mode, and see thoughts, sensations, perceptions, feelings and so on for what they are – fleeting phenomena that do not define you. Meditation can teach us how to detach, and how to reflect on our experience rather than identifying with it, and in doing so, forfeit our ability to consciously choose something different.

Overthinking is endemic. But when we are mindful, we step back from the thought traffic and remind ourselves that *we are not our thoughts*. This should ring bells – it's characteristic of Kegan's stage 4, the self-authoring mind.

Consider an example: you've just received an enormous bill and you're stressed because you don't know how you'll pay it. You get lost in a spiral of anxious overthinking and catastrophizing, being triggered into all sorts of negative self-beliefs and assumptions. "This is such a disaster. Of course this would happen, I've always had bad luck. My life sucks, truly. I'm such an idiot, why don't I have more saved?"

In mindful meditation, you go quiet within and notice all these stories and interpretations flying around your head. These are your core beliefs! You then have a grand realization. There *is* stress and concern. But *you* are not that stress. You are somebody having a temporary experience of stress. The thoughts and beliefs are there, yes, but they will pass. And you can watch them go.

Notice what you cannot bear
We know that core beliefs often take shape in reaction to some initial trauma or negative emotion. We may disown or forget

67

the especially difficult emotions. But this means that, if we're willing to follow these feelings of fear, sadness or shame, instead of avoiding or denying them, they may have a lot to teach us about ourselves, and the core beliefs we are running.

Naturally, we want to resist or avoid our more painful experiences. Humiliation, guilt, deep sadness... these can be hard to hold in awareness. In the moment, it may feel so much easier to be unaware of such unpleasant experiences! We may choose instead to rush in with distractions or, more confusingly, with other emotions that mask over the ones we *really* don't want to face.

Ask yourself, *what core belief is at the root of my wanting to escape/avoid right now?*

In the interests of self-awareness, we can learn to look at these intense negative experiences as a valuable clue, and an invitation to go deeper into awareness. The key here: tolerate the discomfort, instead of fleeing it. You may be surprised at what insights are waiting for you if you can just bear your difficult emotions without denying, avoiding or escaping. Note the task is to bear – you don't have to like it, agree with it, or explain it. Just let it be what it is. Ta da! You have brought the light of awareness into another deep corner of your mind.

If you catch yourself having a strong negative emotion, pause and become aware. Dig down to see what assumptions, expectations, "rules" and beliefs you hold at the bottom of these feelings.

"I can't express my full sadness because if I did, people would find me needy and too much work, and abandon me. So I need to avoid feeling sad at all costs, or I would threaten everything."
This leads to, "I'm only worthy of love if I'm happy and pleasant and undemanding."
This leads to, "I am not enough, as I am."

However, once this core belief has been discovered, your job is not to argue with it or try to stuff it back down again (that will just embed it more firmly in the shadow!). Only become aware. Be curious.

What is the impact of this core belief on your life? How different would life be if you changed it? Learning to tolerate what we think we can't bear (in this example, sadness) is a path to awareness and acceptance. Here, allowing in feelings of sadness could be a relief. As we learn to accept the "intolerable" in ourselves, we find that the world reflects this.

Construct your life timeline
This is an exercise in uncovering core beliefs that will seem simple on the surface, but can be truly eye-opening. Take around twenty minutes with a pen and paper and, beginning from the day of your birth, create a timeline of the major events of your life. Include all the impactful things you can remember, big or small.

Sounds simple, but you may gain a new perspective, when your entire life is laid out on a single page this way. You may see patterns and themes that look so obvious you wonder how you missed them before!

Your core beliefs are there to help organize and connect your disparate life experiences. So, look at your timeline and identify recurrent ideas that you've been using to make sense of these events. What narrative have you constructed about your timeline? What are the core beliefs behind that? Where did they come from?

"I'm an outsider and will never fit in anywhere."
"Life always has a way of sorting itself out, if you have faith."
"It's a woman's job to redeem and 'tame' a man."
"It's us vs. them, and you can never win."
"Artists are not required to worry about money."

It can be especially interesting to notice how your major life events influenced your core beliefs, and how these have changed as you have evolved in maturity and self-awareness. You may have revised your self-concept after a divorce or house move, or had a major epiphany around religion, parenthood, or vocation. Can you see how your current core beliefs are serving you (or not!) in your life right now?

Look at the way you think
Our cognitive distortions can show us a lot about our core beliefs, and our self-awareness. In a way, *every* thought or belief is a kind of distortion, since it colors our immediate perception. However, some beliefs are clearly very inaccurate and negatively impact our lives, especially if we

are unaware that we hold them. The trick is to become aware of them and challenge them. Are we using our cognitive faculties to convince ourselves of some nonsense we have decided is true, or are we using our brainpower to help us understand and engage with the world?

Be honest about your own biases, prejudices and distortions, and allow them to teach you about any ingrained programming you have – so you can change it. For example, you may notice you tend to default to all-or-nothing, black-and-white thinking when you're stressed. If you pause and become aware of this pattern in yourself, you may notice it comes from a cluster of core beliefs you learnt as a child:

Chaos and complexity and nuance is scary and threatening.
I cannot tolerate complexity, because I don't feel in control of it, and I have to be in control. To control complexity, I have to make it less complex. Then everything will be OK.

Now, the awareness of this core belief ("I must be in control") may not make you suddenly abandon it once and for all. You may spend your entire life battling this particular demon. But, you now know this is a part of you, and you can work around it. The next time you're in an argument with someone and hear yourself saying, "well, if you're right, then are you implying I'm wrong?!" you can pause, become aware, and decide in that moment if you want to let that core belief be in the driver's seat. "Well, I suppose both of us could be right. These things can be complicated, and that's OK."

Allow yourself to be triggered
If we're aware, we may notice that our response to any challenging situation is not in fact to that situation at all, but to our memory of something that has happened, long in the past. If we follow these memories, we may unearth some of our deepest assumptions and stories about who we are, and what we can expect from life.

The next time you're triggered, try to determine the original stimulus to which the response belongs. Look at your memories. Notice how your behavior, thoughts and feelings in the present are just automatic reactions to this memory. Are these ideas up-to-date? Are they helping you create the life you want? Are they in any way true or accurate?

In the very instant you are triggered, pause and become aware of the two options ahead of you: you can forfeit your choice and carry on along the same rut as always, responding to the triggering stimulus as you always do, or you can become aware that your reaction is just a bad habit, and can be unlearnt. You can become aware, or even act in another way. Simply doing this immediately empowers you – no longer a victim to your own emotions, they become something you have a say in.

Where is your emotion coming from?
What are you actually feeling?
What core beliefs are running in your mind?
What perspective do you have on this situation?
Are you behaving automatically or are you in conscious control?

Merely by asking these questions, we gain objectivity and stand a little outside our experience, rather than being identified with it.

Own emotions by knowing their names
One very obvious way to gain distance, detachment and objectivity is with words.

By labelling something, we give it a handle for our brain to pick up and examine, separate from ourselves. How can you change or improve on something if you don't even know how to talk about it? How can you own and take responsibility for your experience when you don't quite know how to conceptualize it?

Naming emotions allows you to take a step back from them, but it's also a big part of honestly getting to know yourself. Think of it as emotional literacy – a familiarity with all the fine and subtle shades of different emotions that can arise. We can use psychologist Robert Plutchik's wheel of emotions as a theoretical framework to help us better label and communicate our feelings. Feeling and experiencing an emotion (and wholly identifying with it) is not the same as *knowing you are experiencing it* (i.e. having objective awareness that the emotion is something you "have").

Knowing the names of your emotions doesn't change them, it only shines understanding on what is already occurring. But this is all that's needed to make changes, to accept with honesty and courage, or to communicate our needs to others. Furthermore, you can't hope to be any good at understanding what other people are experiencing unless you have the right vocabulary – how else do we share our internal world except by symbols that point to it?

At the center of the wheel are 8 basic emotions: joy, trust, fear, surprise, sadness, anticipation, anger, and disgust. Just as with a color wheel, where primary colors can be mixed, darkened or lightened, these emotions can vary in intensity. For example, intense fear is terror, while less intense fear is mere apprehension. Anticipation dialed up a notch is vigilance, but toned down it can feel like interest. A mix of joy and trust is said to produce love, while a mixture of annoyance and boredom (diluted versions of anger and disgust) produces the feeling called contempt.

Emotions each have their "opposites" which are positioned on the other side of the wheel. Joy vs. sadness, disgust vs. trust and so on. Each emotion can be said to express itself physiologically, too: when we feel joy, we are compelled to connect, but when we feel sad we tend to do the opposite and withdraw.

When in anticipation we lean in and examine, but when surprised we jump back. Disgust makes us reject whereas trust makes us embrace.

What is the purpose of this wheel? Well, that requires us to understand the purpose of emotions themselves. Emotions are indicators and can draw our attention to what requires more awareness. Think of them as saying, "pay attention to me!" The wheel helps us pay better attention.

Even if you don't agree 100% with the way this emotion wheel has been laid out, it's a good idea to practice emotional literacy by using more words to describe your feelings. Play with describing their intensity, and their combination with other emotions. If it helps, consider first what you feel in your body (a sinking sensation in your gut, the desire to run away, a warmth in your cheeks etc.) and try to refine that into one or two feeling words. Try it right now – close your eyes and ask, *how am I feeling?*

Summary:

- We can improve self-awareness by becoming conscious of our ingrained core beliefs that come from childhood. By understanding the "program" we run, we can make changes and live with more purpose and deliberation.

- We can ask where we first experienced an emotion, and what core beliefs this instilled in us in the past. We can then examine this core belief and look at the effect it has on our lives. Finally, we can ask if we would like to change this belief into something that better helps us create the life we want for ourselves.

- We are often driven by aspects of ourselves that we have pushed out of conscious awareness, i.e. what Jung called the shadow. We heal when we consciously integrate this material, with awareness and acceptance. We know the shadow is at work when we feel unclear about why we act, have disproportionate responses to events, or project onto others.

- There are many simple ways to integrate the shadow, become aware of core beliefs and gently rewrite them. They all rely on awareness.

- We can become aware of what we are most triggered by, and examine who we judge most, to see if we're projecting. We can practice meditation and mindfulness to increase objectivity. By noticing what emotions we feel resistant to, we can practice bearing and accepting them.

- We can also closely examine our cognitive biases and the core beliefs we've picked up during our lives. This goes hand in hand with learning to name and own emotions. Emotional literacy is a way to improve self-awareness and help us get distance from our immediate experience.

Chapter 3: Find your values, big and small

If you've found yourself asking the question "who am I?", you might have also been asking simultaneously, "What should I do?"

Our lack of genuine identity can show itself in an inability to make decisions, to choose a path, to set a goal, or to say what we want—in other words, what we *do* is a reflection of who we *are*. If we have a problem with one, we usually have a problem with the other.

If you're unsure of how to act, you're also probably a little unsure of who you are. Knowing how best to act is a question of knowing what kind of person you are. If you are someone who prioritizes family and social connection above anything else, for example, you don't need to think too hard about the dilemma of working late nights at the office versus spending quality time with your young children. Your identity informs your choices.

In fact, how we respond to life's dilemmas, choices, and difficulties says a lot about the strength of our own values. We are as we do, and we do according to what we value. Inner values and principles are like a personal manifesto that tells us how to act in any situation. This is our own code of ethics that we've devised for ourselves, and it acts like a guiding light even when—or maybe particularly when—the path is unclear.

How shall we define "values"?

A value is a judgment that makes claims about the priorities we hold in life. They are principles, rules, or beliefs that give meaning to our lives. They are what stop life from feeling empty and meaningless, because they are inherently *about* meaning—it's whenever you say, "Thing A is more important and valuable than thing B." In saying this, it follows that the right thing to do is thing A.

Values not only guide our action when we're unclear, they give us strength to carry on when the path might be clear but the journey difficult. You might have a really difficult time turning down those extra hours at work, but when you can tune into the deeper value of being present in your children's lives as they grow up, you are given strength to make a decision that makes you unpopular at work.

Granted, many of the values you might hold, consciously or unconsciously, are secondhand. They come to us from our cultures, our parents, our religion, our political environment, even our historical era. Some values might be held uncritically, i.e. you may have them simply out of habit, and haven't really examined them closely. Others might be personally chosen after extensive deliberation. Values can change over time. We might rebel against the values of our group, accept them completely, or negotiate a little, but we always have the option to be more conscious and deliberate about our own values. If you were put on the spot right now and asked what your values were, how quickly and easily do you think you could answer? Do you think you could easily list five or ten of the things you most value in life? Going even further, could you say confidently that your life mostly aligns with these values? It's one thing to *know* what's right, but there's very little point in devising a complete book of rules that you never really intend to follow.

Don't Choose Your Core Values, Clarify Them

Though the self-help industry might sometimes have you believe otherwise, your identity isn't just something you go shopping for like you do a pair of sneakers or a brand of shampoo. You cannot just pick and choose values—they need to be a *genuine* expression of what you really do care about. This can seem a little like a catch-22 situation—you don't have an identity so you need to find your values, but how do you know which values you care about without having an identity?

The process is not as difficult as it seems.

Firstly, know that the process isn't done all at once—you are not going to uncover a complete and fully-functioning self in an afternoon and start living your best life once you wake up tomorrow morning. It's a *process*, and insight will come in fits and starts. In fact, a life well-loved might be one in which you continually revisit the question of identity, with your answers deepening on every attempt.

We also need to remember that, in finding values, we are the ultimate arbiters. We decide. So, you might need to take the time to tune out every other voice so you can better hear your own. There is no wrong way to do it. There's no right answer. There's only what works for *you*.

Having said that, people are motivated by a lot of different values, which it might help to consider in finding out our own:

Financial independence or wealth

Being in nature

Romantic love or connection with others

Having freedom and independence

Learning and knowledge

Fun and adventure

Good physical health and fitness

Spiritual or religious pursuits

Art and creativity

Work accomplishments, leadership, business

Security and survival

Social cohesion and harmony in a group

Peace, calm, and contentment; relaxation

Honor, loyalty, and dependability

. . . and so on.

You might look at all of the above and think that they're all valuable. But the trick is in identifying your *priorities*—those things that are best, that bring the most satisfaction and meaning. You may care about creative expression and individuality,

86

but your love of family stability may trump that ten times over. You need to know how each of your needs and preferences rank relative to each another.

A good way to find out what matters most is to ask what has seemingly bought you the most happiness and sense of meaning in the past. If you look at all your high points in life, and they all involved adventure and freedom to travel and explore, that tells you something. It works the other way around too: in thinking of your life's most painful memories, why did they hurt so much? Could it be that these events were moments when your deepest values were disappointed or violated? Tally up the achievements you're genuinely proud of and see what they have in common. Or, look more closely at your worst failures and blunders and ask why they stung particularly badly—were these times where you acted *against* your values?

Another trick is to look at the people you admire or wish to be like (or even envy)—what values do they exemplify? If all your role models and heroes are self-made entrepreneurs, is this telling you about the value you place on financial independence? Maybe. Or maybe what appeals to you about them is that they're unique and following their own dreams, breaking the rules. Or maybe they are reflecting your yearning for a life filled with more admiration and recognition.

Since you are uncovering your values rather than creating them from scratch, another general technique is to look at all the decisions you are currently making—they may speak strongly to values you might not yet be aware you actually have. Watch yourself closely for a few days or a week, and notice your decisions when faced with a choice to make. Notice how you feel when you choose one thing over another.

It might be that you notice yourself often choosing things that leave you feeling bad, and don't really feel aligned with who you are. It may be that you notice key decisions reflecting your values. Either way, we are already living by values every moment of every day—it's simply a question of becoming aware of them and asking whether they're the choices that best reflect the values we hold—or want to hold.

Look for patterns. See if you can find any strong feelings one way or another—are there any non-negotiable sentiments? What are you absolutely unwilling to do or give up? Why? What choices make you feel proud and content, and which ones feel like a compromise, an obligation, or even something you're embarrassed about?

Feeling right, however, is just one aspect that helps determine your values. You also need to make informed decisions about what you really believe in that rely on more than just your emotional inclinations at any given time. Say you're confused about whether you value your career or your connection with friends and family more. You've found that abandoning your family for work often leaves you feeling guilty, and so you think maybe you value your family more than your career. The next step here is to try to find out *why* you feel that way. There can be many factors external to yourself that are influencing this feeling of guilt. Maybe you just have FOMO (fear of missing out), or your family has ingrained a value system in you that says work should always come second.

To get a clearer picture of what valuing something really entails, it helps to read a little on the various reasons why one might want to prioritize something over the other. We are rarely aware of all the reasons one or the other might be a good idea. Just a few searches will yield several reasons for either choice. When reading these, don't just think about which reasons sound more appealing, think about what feels *right* to you. These will often have a lot to do with what your goals in life are. Are you really ready to sacrifice personal success to have a stronger bond with your family? Or would you rather focus on your career while ensuring your family is important, but not paramount? Thinking in this way will prevent you from repeating the earlier cycle of simply having imbibed certain values from your surroundings without really considering what matters most to *you*.

Values (and the identity that comes with them) are not abstract. They are real, lived things, out there in the world. They express themselves in actions and choices. True, they may not always be expressed perfectly all the time. But the *intention* is to live by them. They are a yardstick by which to measure your life, whether you achieve that standard or not. This is why it's more effective to look at your actual life in action when considering values, rather than just sitting down with a piece of paper and pulling nice-sounding ideas out of your imagination. Remember, we are striving for the *real* self, and not just another false self.

What About My Goals?

Be honest with yourself. In asking what you value, you are halfway on the road to knowing who you are, and when you know who you are, you know how to act, and why. In trying to find your identity, you might be tempted to start thinking about your goals in life. But this is premature. You can only decide on your goals when you know what you value (and don't value!). How many of us have chosen a goal, only to reach it and realize it isn't what we really wanted, or it doesn't have the desired effect on us? It's probably because we didn't stop to think whether our goals actually lined up with our values.

Goals are important, but they emerge from our values—not the other way around. Yes, your interests and preferences matter. Your obligations and commitments matter. You need to make plans and understand your strengths and weaknesses. But all of this comes after you do the important work of setting up your values. Without them, you cannot undertake any other task with clarity, and you will have that nagging sense of aimlessness in your life—no matter how many impressive-sounding goals you come up with.

When we have our values clearly identified within us, it's as though life is suddenly clearly outlined, and we can see what is inside that outline and what is outside. We know what is relevant to us, and what is a distraction or a diversion. We know how to assess things, and how to measure our actions. We know where we're going and what we stand for. And all of this adds up to a life that feels *purposeful*. We don't feel wishy-washy or unsure of ourselves— instead, our identify firmly takes shape, and we are consciously aware of who we are and what we're doing. It's very simple: we cannot be fulfilled if we don't have values. Without values, we have nothing to compare our achievements against, and all our actions feel pointless. With values, however, life just flows so much more smoothly.

Consider an example. Someone might work hard to discover that their primary value in life is spiritual enrichment. Looking at their lives, they see how so much of their joy has come from reading spiritual and religious texts, volunteering, going to retreats, meditating, and taking plenty of time to be in nature, where they feel closest to the divine.

Because this value is strongly identified, it acts as a guiding force for everything in this person's life. When they're feeling depressed, they know to stop and ask, "Am I neglecting my spiritual needs? How can I reconnect to that feeling that sustains me and gives me hope?" When faced with a conflict with themselves or with others, they fall back on their code of ethics that comes from their values—they approach problems with compassion, forgiveness, and a little humor.

When they're standing in the checkout line at the supermarket and they see a trashy tabloid paper with a cover designed to inflame and aggravate, this person is able to stop, take a breath, and say, is this me? Is that who I want to be? Then they can turn away and choose not to engage with that kind of material in their life. What you eat and drink, what you say, where you live, the work you do, the clothes you wear—all of this reflects who you are and what you value. In this way, both big and small value decisions create a framework and a foundation for an entire life. When clarified this way, you can see how powerful it is to know one's own values.

Here's the thing: you already have values. Whether you got them from your family, your society, or Instagram, you have them. Whether you're aware of them or not, they're there, guiding your life. So why not make sure the values you have are something you consciously want?

We need to be careful that we are always tuning in to the *real self*, and not another *false self*. How many times have we heard about the person having a midlife crisis, or a teenager going through "a phase"? They seem to be trying on a few costumes in the attempt to settle on one that fits. People in these transitional states of life may cling to an identity they think they *should* have, or wished they did have, but it is still not a genuine reflection of who they are. This work takes patience, honesty, and a little determination (and yes, you may need to go through a few awkward "phases" yourself on the way!).

Now that we've seen what value-discovery *isn't* (it's not about goals, other people's opinions, or switching out one false self for another one), we can look more closely at what it is. Here's a step-by-step guide to bring you closer.

Value Clarification, Step by Step

STEP ONE: CLEAR YOUR MIND

If we wish to fill ourselves up with something new, we first need to pour out all the old that's already there, and start fresh. We need to let go of any bias, expectations, or preconceived notions. Being fixed in our thinking, we can imagine we already know the answer to everything—but this understandably undermines the process of discovery. You really need to trust that there is something for you to learn, something unknown out there that you are willing to encounter openly.

It's difficult, but try to drop (at least temporarily) any preconceived ideas about who you are. Your conscious mind may want to jump in and tell you a narrative ("you're an introvert, you're a worrier, you're XYZ"), but set these aside and give some space for your unconscious mind to come to the fore and see new possibilities. We have all been taught which values are "better" than others—we need to forget this lesson if we want to find our *own* values for ourselves!

STEP TWO: START A LIST

Remember that values aren't chosen, they're clarified. Trust that you already have them, you just have to *discover* them. You don't want to inadvertently write down a list of all the things that other people expect you to be.

Scan the list given earlier and see if any of them spark your interest. If not quite, how could you tweak them so they seem more valuable in your opinion? When compiling a list, start broadly and don't censor yourself. Add anything that strikes you as important. You might begin by writing "love," but on further reflection, tease that out a bit more. What kind of love, and why? You might decide that what you really value is brotherly love, friendships, belonging to a community. You could then put "community" on the list and see if that spurs any further values.

As you go, draw on both your best and worst life memories to guide you, as described above. The moments you felt most yourself—what was happening, and what were you doing? The moments when you felt frustrated, violated, disappointed, or uncomfortable—what was not happening, and what does this tell you about the feelings you hold dear?

You might recall the greatest day of your life so far, the birth of your first child. In thinking about why this felt so amazing, you jot a few more notes on your list. You realize that you felt a deep, deep sense of purpose knowing that you now had someone to look after. You examine those feelings of hope, of dedication, of amazement. You realize that being a parent satisfies some of your core values—selfless love, belonging, trust, and hope for the future.

Ask yourself questions to dig closer toward those things in life that bring a sense of meaning. What makes a good day good? What makes you proud and grateful? What makes life worth living (i.e. you'd be miserable without it)? Look not only at the standards you hold for yourself, but those you hold for others. What is a deal breaker for you in your relationships? What is your idea of a person *not* living a meaningful and purposeful life?

STEP THREE: PULL IT ALL TOGETHER

Eventually, you should have a long list of things you value. Though all of these things are important, they can probably be distilled down to a few *main* core values. Read over the notes you've made and see if you can group them into chunks. For example, "community," "friendship," and "compassion for others" have a lot in common, as do "independence," "freedom to follow my own path," and "part-time employment."

Remember, you are not judging anything you have on the list. If you genuinely identify it as a value, put it down. If, on further reflection, you really don't care all that much about innovation or winning awards, then leave them out. As you work (without attachment or judgment!), you should start seeing some clarity emerge. As much as you can, try to connect these ideas to real life—are these values you've actually experienced before meaningful, or have you just been raised or socialized to assume that you want them?

Once you have some clusters of values, see if you can dig deep and identify the main theme uniting them all. In our examples above, friendship, compassion, and community all have one thing in common: the joy of shared human connection. Take your time with this—what is it, really, that makes all of the things on your list so appealing to you?

STEP FOUR: RANK YOUR VALUES

Some people might find that, even after clustering, they're still left with a big list. But, life is filled with choices, and since we are limited, we are often called on to choose between two important and worthwhile things. This is why we need to clarify further and prioritize our values.

You now want to whittle down to those essential values that you absolutely cannot live without. The most fundamental, most basic needs of yours, without which you'd be completely lost, miserable, or pointless. Even if you can identify a few of these, try to choose between five and ten values that you feel neatly capture the dimensions of what's most important to you.

Then, rank them in order of importance. You might do this in ten minutes or find you need a few days to really contemplate it deeply. Use your feelings as a guide, and remember not to rush—you are setting aside everything you know about your false self so that you can meet the acquaintance of your real self—that takes time!

STEP FIVE: LET YOUR VALUES COME ALIVE

If you write something like "physical health and fitness" as a core value, it may seem a little abstract. Time to embed this sentiment out in the real world and put it into context! You want to put these newly discovered core values into a shorthand form that will inspire you every time you look at it, and remind you precisely of the best things in life—according to your most authentic self.

For the person valuing physical fitness, a single beautiful image of a ballet dancer in a powerful leaping pose, mid-flight, might capture the essence of what you value so much: pushing against the limits of human physicality to find beauty and expression in the joy of having a living, moving body. Or, you might find that a certain phrase or quote captures your core value better, a bit like a mission statement. Find a stimulus that triggers a strong emotional reaction— it's these emotions that point you in the right direction and speak more directly to your inner self than any dry, abstract language could.

STEP SIX: TRY THEM ON FOR SIZE

No, you're not done quite yet! Value discovery is an ongoing process. Once you've identified and condensed your core values, see how they fit out in real life. Leave the list for a while and come back to it, seeing how it feels. Do you feel comfortable, in alignment, and clear . . . or are some things still not quite feeling like "you"? Look for the hidden voice of your parents, your culture, etc., and ask whether they've been swaying your list or the way you rank things. If your intuition pipes up, listen to what it says. This may sometimes feel like vague, flimsy work, but rest assured that you are exploring exciting new realms that many people never give themselves permission to enter.

And that's that. Your core values distilled into a concentrated essence that tells you a lot about who you are as a person, and helps you answer a range of questions from, "What should I do?" to, "What do I want right now?"

Putting Your Values to Work

Of course, values aren't just things you "have." Discovering your values is about so much more than simply creating a list. **Your identity is what results when you express your values in the world**. In other words, a consistently lived value becomes identity.

Once you have comfortably identified a core value list that makes you happy, you need to do the hard work of asking how well you actually manifest this value in your own life. Many people claim that they value their families and children more than anything, but anyone could look at their life and see that on the ground, that person doesn't spend any time at home, forgets their kids' birthdays, and just recently spent their college money on a sports car.

That person may truly value their family, but their actions are badly out of alignment with that value. It's time for you to see how much these values are actually appearing in your own life. When you are faced with a choice, do you actually behave like a person who holds the values you claim to? If you've placed one value as a priority over all others, is that actually reflected in the amount of time, money, and energy you spend on it?

A great way to do this is to actually draw up a chart. Put all your values in a column on the left, and in a column on the right, rate from one to ten your level of satisfaction on this value. If you prize art, beauty, and poetic expression, for example, do you feel that this need/value of yours is in reality fulfilled? Rate all your values this way, remembering that you want to be honest and judgmental—no point in lying to yourself or pretending.

You can probably guess what this list will allow you to do next. Take a look at your ratings. For the lowest ranking, can you write down, in a third column, some concrete actions you can take to bring that value more into your life? If you can do this, you might notice something magical—you have suddenly given yourself a smart, data-driven way to answer the question, "What should I do and what do I want from life?" You already know that if you take action toward any of these unfulfilled values, you are guaranteed to increase your sense of meaning and purpose. What a powerful tool to have!

From *here*, you can begin to turn your mind to goals. The goals you make from this point in the process will be properly informed by what truly matters to you in your life. Let's say you notice that you value knowledge and learning, but are embarrassed to find that, even though you've ranked it as one of your top three values, you can't even remember the last time you did something to satisfy that need. You immediately set some goals for yourself: you sign up for a philosophy course, buy a few fun novels and commit to a daily reading quota, or sign up to learn a skill or craft you've always wanted to learn. These actions might feel a little scary, especially if you are taking a big step out of your comfort zone, but they should in a broad sense feel *right*—they should feel like you are taking the right step in the right direction.

Keep this chart somewhere safe, and return to it in a few weeks or months to check on your progress. How do you rate your expression and fulfillment of a certain value now, after achieving some goals? What adjustments can you make? Don't be too surprised to find that you need to reorder your values or drop a few completely. Sometimes, only practical experience will teach us what is real and what is just illusion. This is something to celebrate—as you fine tune your list, you are getting closer and closer to your genuine self, and trimming away at the false self.

Your Values: A Powerful Decision-Making Tool

As we've seen, values are living things; they are practical, action-based principles. And one of the most practical ways to bring them to life is to allow them to guide and shape your decision-making process. There are two ways to do this. The first is to ask yourself, "How would a person with my values behave in this situation?"

For example, you're someone whohas discovered that you derive enormous satisfaction and meaning out of being diligent, hard working, and dedicated. You feel proud when you start something and finish it, no matter what. You are happiest when you think of yourself as someone who follows through, and who keeps their word. You value integrity.

Along comes a choice one day. In this case, it's just a small choice: the decision between cutting corners on a project where it won't really matter, or doing a proper, complete job even though it would take a little more time and energy. If you value integrity, the right choice is obvious: you do the job well. Not because of the external rewards or pressures, but because you already know that *you* value doing a good job. Naturally, if you were a different person with different values, the "right" choice might be exactly the opposite one.

The second way to use values to help with decision-making is to consciously imagine the *outcome* of certain choices in the future, and then weigh up this outcome against your list of prioritized values. This works a little better for bigger decisions that play out in the long term. For example, you might be wondering whether to accept a new job offer.

You carefully imagine what your life would look like one, two, or five years in the future if you accept this offer. You try to imagine all the effects this will have on your finances, your family life, your lifestyle in general, your career, and so on. Take your time exploring this potential future. Now, from this position, inside your future vision, take another look at your values list. Living your future life, does your satisfaction rating for any of your values go up or down?

Maybe you see that your financial situation would improve, but actually, financial wealth is not a value on your list. You notice also that the new job would have you move further away from family, and spend more time in the office. This would negatively affect your identified value of family time, parenting, and a happy home life. On the other hand, your future self will also experience a boost in occupational fulfillment—which is on your list.

So, what decision do you make? Because you have ranked your values, you can see that career achievement is important to you, but it's not as important as a happy family life. So, your decision is made. You don't take the job. You do this with full knowledge not just of how the job will affect you, but how it will affect your values. You know that the choice you make is one that brings you closer to your fulfilled, properly aligned, and contented self, and further away from a false self (i.e. the one that knows that the job is "once in a lifetime" and that all your friends will think you're crazy for turning it down . . .)

It's likely that you will have some values that conflict with each other. Like the person who values his family but ignores them nonetheless, we can value our career and family both at the same time. In such cases, a simple ranking won't always help us. We might *generally* value one over the other, but that does not mean we should choose the thing we value more every single time. This is true even when we don't have value conflicts like these. Decision-making is an active process; we can't simply compile certain values and rely on a ranking to have every choice pre-decided for us. While a ranking chart is a good general guide to what we should do, we still need to make decisions on a case-by-case basis.

Coming back to the value conflict, the best way to resolve this clash is to take a balanced approach. You can prioritize family on some occasions, and your career on others. If there is something preventing you from doing this, maybe your time management, attempt to work on those issues so that you don't feel like you're skimping on one thing you value for another.

The examples we've discussed here are necessarily small and quite simple. But it's hard to overstate just how much your life can change when you apply your values list consistently. When you are guided by your core values, you have a certain gravity and weight to your character. You have direction and purpose. You can more easily bear difficulty and are more resilient because your energy and attention is focused on one point, rather than being diffuse and reactive.

It may seem like a simple solution, but in the end, we are what we value. A well-considered values list is a tool that clarifies our will and intention, motivates and inspires us, and keeps us going in difficult or confusing times. By now you can probably see that the problem we call "not knowing yourself" is more accurately the problem of "not knowing what you care about."

Summary

- A value is a rule, principle, or belief that gives meaning to your life. It is usually something you consider very important in life and base many of your decisions around. This is why when you're confused about what to do in a certain situation or circumstances that you find yourself in, the cause is usually a lack of clarity on what your real values are.
- If you're not sure what your values are in life, don't worry; discovering them is not hard. However, the process does take time, and you won't simply wake up tomorrow with complete knowledge of what your values are.
- The first step to discovering what your values are is to simply abandon all preconceived notions you have of who you are. Often, the values we have been living by are actually derived externally. This can be through our family, culture,

111

historical era, etc. By starting from a clean slate, we avoid such influences from clouding our judgment regarding our true values.

- Next, think about the things that you feel most strongly about. This could be personal success, close family bonds, serving others in the form of social work, etc. Finding one will often lead you to other values you hold because they point to a "higher" value you possess. Thus, valuing family over career means that your interpersonal relationships in general are valuable to you.

- Once you have a complete list of values, think about your goals in life and how your values align with them. Are the things you're doing now in conjunction with your values and goals? If not, think of ways you can change that and live a life that is truer to your real self.

- As you discover your values, doing actions that promote them will help you decide what it is that you really consider important.

Chapter 4: We don't talk anymore!

Your core beliefs about yourself (chapter 2) and your deepest held values and principles (chapter 3) are primarily about *internal* self-awareness, or our ability to know who we are, what we want, and what we think, and what we feel. In the second half of this book, however, we remember that introspection and awareness of your internal landscape is only one half of the picture – what about *external* self-awareness?

Mature, developed adults with healthy emotional intelligence cannot help but be socially aware, too. This means they have empathy, good communication skills, and the ability to consider other people's unique needs. They can happily take on feedback, praise and criticism from others, and genuinely consider other people's perspectives. They can manage conflict, cooperate, share, and understand others despite their differences. This may remind you of the "socialized mind" from Kegan's 5 stages, but the fully developed person is not just about imitating their culture's social norms – they're good at balancing *both* internal and external self-awareness.

Using conversation to learn about yourself

Have you ever considered that conversation could be a form of introspection?

Conventional self-reflection has been shown to correlate with higher anxiety, depression and a host of other negative outcomes. Though insight predicts greater wellbeing, better relationships and higher self-knowledge, introspection doesn't lead to insight. In other words, thinking about yourself isn't the same as knowing about yourself. Though conventional wisdom hails introspection as the path to self-knowledge, it can more often cloud our perception, make us fixate on the negative, and have us swamped in our own emotions, feeling powerless.

This is perhaps because we're doing introspection wrong. The worst offender? Leading with *why* questions.

When we ask *why*, confirmation bias and other assumptions mean we grab hold of any idea that seems to fit, aimlessly misleading ourselves. *Why* keeps you in the past, and keeps you a victim. This question seems so natural on the surface, but when you fixate on *why*, you pave the way for rationalizations and distortions. If you focus instead on *what* questions, you open yourself to discovering new information. Tasha Eurich and colleagues from Chapter 1 found that this simple switch from *why* to *what* was the biggest predictor of high self-awareness.

For example, you could ask, "why am I so upset right now?" and respond with "because of that stupid idiot who's always pushing my buttons!" See how nothing has changed? That no additional self-awareness is gained?

If you ask instead, "what am I feeling right now? What's going on with me?" you may have the chance to gain insight into the situation. You are now open to possibilities.

You are primed to see your choice in the matter, too.

Now, let's zoom out and consider the one activity in life most supportive of asking these kinds of questions – conversations. Instead of endless loops of navel-gazing and self-absorption, you can use dialogue (with yourself and others) as an infinitely more sophisticated method for discovering more about yourself. Think of it as the difference between a person sitting in a dark room, alone, talking to themselves, and the person in a conversation with someone else, actively exchanging perspectives and ideas – who is more likely to be self-aware?

The art of questioning yourself

Imagine you make a bad mistake one day and, in frustration, you ask yourself, "what on earth is wrong with me?"

Sure, it's just a hypothetical question, but think about the possible answers anyway: what's wrong with you? Well, I guess you're bad in some way. You're a moron. Whatever it is, the question is drawing attention directly to your flaws. Not helpful, right? Look deeper though: the question assumes that there is a flaw. Notice that if you ask this question, it's impossible to arrive at the answer "it was a simple accident, don't worry about it." It's also more difficult to find your way to a potential solution to the problem you've created.

This is to say that whenever we are learning more about ourselves, we are always engaging on two levels – we are looking at the world from within our mindset or stage of awareness, and we also question that world itself, from the outside. Objective and subjective, detached and identified.

Now, questions can operate on either level. Let's say you have a hammer and believe that every problem you encounter can be fixed with the right hammer. You encounter a problem and ask, "what kind of hammer do I need here?" This question might help you, but one thing it can never do is shed light on how accurate your hammer philosophy is – or make you aware that you are using it at all!

You may one day encounter a problem that will only be solved when you can ask yourself, "what tool do I need to fix this?" (Notice again that the *what* question will be infinitely more helpful than the *why* question. Why doesn't a hammer work to fix a problem that needs a screwdriver? Well, because it just doesn't. Unpicking *why* would be a weird rabbit hole to fall into).

Every conversation or dialogue is an opportunity to expand awareness, see blind spots and broaden understanding. And that includes your conversations with yourself! As we've seen, though, it turns out there is such a thing as a stupid question – or, to put it more kindly, some questions will keep you trapped within the problem that generated that question, and others will help show you something beyond the state of mind you're asking from. We need to commit ourselves to asking the best questions of ourselves, and then answering honestly and deeply.

So, what questions are the right ones to ask? (Aha! Now *there's* a high-quality question). You can never receive an answer of a caliber higher than the question you are asking, so pay attention to crafting questions that push right to the edge of your understanding. The exact questions you ask can be infinite. But they will fall into broad categories, according to the purpose they serve. Think of self-awareness as the result of a kind of auto-therapy, where you become an expert at conversing with yourself. Let's look more closely:

Clarity questions

Big idea: WHAT IS?

Imagine a team of researchers who want to set about understanding more about language delays in bilingual children in a particular area. They've designed a huge program to help support kids' learning needs, they're funded by dozens of concerned charities, and they're all ready to go… until their studies find some confusing results and the thing comes grinding to a halt: apparently, there are no language delays. Oops.

You cannot set goals, make plans, or correct faults if you poorly understand what you're dealing with, right now. Many of us breeze past our own assumptions and expectations, never noticing the enormous conclusions we've jumped to or the grand overarching theories we're taking as a given, with zero evidence.

Perhaps the most important question to ask at first is the kind that will help you understand what is happening, what you are looking at, and the situation, internally and externally. As far as possible, you want to see a clear vision of reality *before* you put a filter, interpretation or judgment on it. If you are rushing in with assumptions, you are not perceiving, but obliviously repeating a mental habit from the past. From this viewpoint, learning is an impossibility. You'll lack self-awareness, and life will feel confusing.

Too many of us start with questions that already contain hidden orders, wishes, or desires, and we don't realize that we've narrowed our own field of possibility. Instead, take it as your first goal to merely *perceive what is*, as fully as possible. This includes the internal and external world you are inhabiting. For example:

What expectations, assumptions or beliefs do I hold about relationships?
What am I feeling right now?
What is my role and responsibility in creating the situation?
How am I defining my current experience?

What is the perspective of other people in this scenario?

What is the simplest, most concise way to describe what is happening?

What core beliefs are activated right now?

How would someone else appraise this situation?

Is there a difference between my experience and those of others?

As you can see, these questions are all versions of the same uber-question: what is?

Crafting a good question takes more effort and thought than it first appears. Before you even answer it, know how the question itself is framed. Does it contain a covert assumption or a strong hint to the answer you're looking for? A great question to ask yourself repeatedly is: *is this question helping?*

This invites a degree of metacognition, as you question the questioning process itself. But remember, your goal is not to get lost in endless philosophizing that leads nowhere (except, perhaps, to a panic attack). Remember Kegan's theory and remember that questions, ideas, models, attitudes, interpretations and theories are all just things you can *have*. Look at them as tools and become curious about the results they're generating. Ask a range of questions and be as honest as possible.

Imagine you have learned of certain illegal activities your colleagues are involved in at work, but have been told to keep quiet, implicating you. Your colleagues claim it's common practice anyway, and you would risk earning a bad reputation if you called attention to it. You discover that several of your immediate managers are even involved. You don't know what to do. Eventually, you're asked to do something you know is wrong. The question is urgent: should you do it or not?

This is a good question to ask, but others will help provide more clarity, such as:

What are my ultimate core values and principles in life?
What am I being asked to do here and who does it serve?
What effect will participating have on my life and career?
What do I genuinely think and feel about this job, and my colleagues?

If you only focused on whether you should or shouldn't, you'd miss out on so many dimensions to the situation, and would not allow yourself to act from full, conscious intention and self-awareness.

Possibility questions

Big idea: WHAT IS POSSIBLE?

As humans, we can't seem to resist noticing what *could be* every time we look at *what is*.

If you can clearly perceive what is happening in the moment, then you are also simultaneously seeing what is not happening. And from there it's just a small jump to the next big question: what is possible here?

This lies at the root of every problem-solving endeavor. You can see how things are, but could they be some other way? What if...?

This question is, naturally, one to ask only after you've gathered as accurate perception of the current reality as possible. Again, we can see how important it is to gain objectivity and to step back from concepts, thoughts, feelings, beliefs and assumptions.

Because when we do, we realize something profound: they are not 100% fixed and unchangeable. Something else could be the case. In this frame of mind, you are in the realm of inventors, artists, explorers and science fiction authors!

Here, we also exercise restraint and resist barging ahead with a premature solution or conclusion. We need to be comfortable with uncertainty, and not get too attached to any one possibility over another – we're just brainstorming, as they say. This is the time where we look at our beliefs and ask if they're true, or where we turn our most stubbornly held assumptions upside down to see if the perspective shift creates any new insights.

What could this situation evolve into?
How can I think differently from how I'm thinking right now?
What could I do to elevate this situation, or raise the standard?
What if the things I'm thinking are impossible aren't?
What aspects have I ignored or downplayed?
If there were no limits, what could I create here?

124

Asking these questions, we sometimes realize: that we held the answers to a problem inside us all along. Problem-solving is often a question of just learning what we already know.

Here's a very simple example. You may have written a grocery shopping list and headed to the store with a very specific idea of the meals you would prepare in the next few days. You get to the store and half of what you want isn't available. The question "what is?" can be answered pretty quickly, but what about what could be? Many of us dwell on sudden changes of plan, failures, setbacks and obstacles to such an extent that we don't notice we are in a perfectly workable situation right now, it's just not the one we were expecting.

"What *is* available and what meals could I prepare with these ingredients?"
"What could I buy to substitute for these ingredients?"
"What are my other options for getting the ingredients I need? Other stores? Eating out tonight? A grocery home delivery?"
"What if I decided not to eat any more and instead manufactured chlorophyll so I could photosynthesize like a plant? I'd save so

much money!" (Ok this last one is silly, but creative thinking never hurt anyone! This line of thinking might spur you to realize that you could make significant savings by eating less...).

Intention questions

Big idea: WHAT DO I WANT?

You've looked at what is, and you've considered what could be. Out of the (sometimes infinite) set of possibilities that can branch off from this present moment, which one do you desire? Which one accords best with your deepest held core values? Which ones are in your control? What precisely can you do to bring about your chosen future, and what do those actions look like, every step of the way?

Humans have a double blessing – we possess the ability to become conscious of ourselves and our environment, *and* we can take actions to deliberately change both. But the first is necessary for the second to occur.

Once you know what you're dealing with and what else is possible, you can use questions to help you apply your own will and

126

intention to reality, to help shape and steer it towards the outcome you want. High external self-awareness, as we've seen, means we may comply with societal expectations and conventions. But only when we combine it with high internal self-awareness, can we use our innate morality and values to guide our actions.

This means it is possible to be a person who is very motivated and goal-oriented, even successful, but who nevertheless lacks insight or self-awareness. This is because they have merely adopted the conventional values as their own. If you are not in the habit of asking on a deep level what you want, what you can create, and who you are, you may take actions that don't fit with your highest values, and don't ultimately fulfill you. Perhaps you become like those "successful" people in high-powered, respectable careers who are nevertheless miserable and have no idea who they are deep-down.

Intention questions are those that help pull our focus onto what we can personally do, what action we can take, and our scope of agency. Some people are deeply introspective, insightful and self-aware of the subtleties of every situation they find themselves in, but they rarely ask themselves how they would like to change that situation, and into what they could change it. They never ask themselves what they can **do** to solve the problem, and so they often don't!

What kind of a person are my actions making me into?
What can I change here and what is out of my control?
What is the one best thing I can do right now to improve my situation?
What kind of life do I want to live, and what kind of person do I want to be?
What would I like to create?
What am I doing to maintain the status quo? How am I responsible?
What unique gifts and perspectives can I share and contribute to the world?

Let's say you're a woman who has been fighting with her boyfriend for pretty much the entire relationship. You may be completely in subjective, passive, reactive mode, and constantly ask questions like, "why me? Why does he treat me this way? Why are relationships so hard? Why doesn't he love me?" and so on. You look at your relationship, which makes you utterly miserable, and you almost see it as a force of nature you are merely at the mercy of. You do only complain bitterly.

Nothing changes; nothing improves. One day you see a therapist who asks you a question that shatters your world, in the best way possible: "why are you creating this for yourself?" You can't stop thinking about it. Weren't you the victim? Wasn't your boyfriend the one doing all the creating? But the more you think about it, the more you get in touch with what you *want*. You focus on what could be. Not the injustice of the situation, or the minute psychological details, or the endless but impotent analyzing you could potentially do…

You are no longer thinking of the situation in terms of your boyfriend and what *he* wants, or how bad you feel, or who's to blame, or how you could force him to be someone he clearly isn't. Instead, you focus on your immense power to actively change the situation. This is a powerful subject-object shift.

You sit down with a pen and paper and go wild writing down everything you **want**. You realize that you have forfeited your own agency, and your innate right to steer your life and create the conditions of your happiness. You can set goals. You can speak up, take action, create. You realize, too, that you were becoming a resentful, apathetic person – and that was not the character you wanted to create for yourself! The next day, you break up.

You can apply the above three question types to a situation you are in, or you can use them after the fact, to better understand something that's already occurred. Either way, take your time, ask more questions rather than fewer, and stay curious. Try to remember that your questions are there to help you gain clarity, identify possibilities, and then consciously and purposely act to bring about the outcome that most serves you.

Clarity questions are perfect for enhancing internal self-awareness.
Possibility and intention questions are good for developing external self-awareness, and helping you synthesize internal and external.

Using questions in self-conversation

There are many ways to begin using smart questions to learn more about yourself (as opposed to getting caught in an introspection loop that goes nowhere). Ideally, each of us would have unlimited access to sagely elders who could engage in generative dialogue to help us uncover the deeper truths about ourselves. But for most of us, we have to make do with artificially constructing this healthy dialogue ourselves. This can be done by writing down pointed questions and taking the time to carefully answer them. How?

Structure journal entries like conversations, with a new line for the character you're speaking to. This character can be an imaginary friend, a person from history, God or an angel, your "higher self," your future or past self, a totem animal or mythical creature that is personally meaningful, a teacher or spiritual leader, your shadow, a completely neutral and disinterested third party, or a role model you know in real life.

Begin with clarity questions and open up a space for dialogue, reminding yourself that you will be on the lookout for knee-jerk judgment, ego, assumptions and biases. If you like, create mind maps, sketches or art to help you contemplate the themes you're engaging with. You could mix up written contemplation with a literal, out-loud conversation. Address an imaginary person in the room, a stuffed animal, your reflection in the mirror, or whatever else seems appropriate.

As you talk or write, remember the difference between objective and subjective, and try to reframe any *why* questions as *what* questions. To prevent yourself from going down rabbit holes of self-absorption, routinely ask if your reflection is going anywhere. Here's a good test: your analysis should lead to transformation, new goals, clarity, insight or a definite plan of action. At some point, you should make a decision to **act**. If you only find it makes you dwell on negative feelings, feel powerless or deepen any confirmation bias, it's time for some radical honesty!

Once you've gained some clarity on the situation, start to explore possibilities. Look at cause and effect, and stay focused on what your scope of action is – and isn't. For example, draw three columns and list out what you can change, what you cannot change, and what you can change but only to a certain degree.

This will help you naturally lead onto questions of intention, and deciding how you want to use action to bring about the reality you most desire. With regular reflection, journaling, or self-conversation, you should confidently and comfortably arrive at the insight that compels you to act. You may wish to set yourself a goal, or re-strategize on your current plan for achieving that goal. Perhaps you need to rethink certain core beliefs, or that your situation is best improved with some very straightforward concrete action, right now.

Whatever it is, be patient. Self-awareness is not something that can be rushed, forced or faked. If you do not genuinely experience an inner transformation, it's impossible to pretend! So, if you're not experiencing mind-blowing insights and epiphanies as quickly as you'd like, relax. Become curious about your resistance, confusion or discomfort, rather than getting irritated with it.

Let's imagine an example. Picture Anna, whose best friend Leah is about to get married. One day, she learns that Leah's fiancé actually has a very questionable financial background, replete with bankruptcies, tax evasion and even suggestions of fraud, now been swept under the carpet. Anna doesn't know, however, if Leah knows any of this. Unsure whether she should bring it up before the wedding, she consults another friend, Natalie, for advice – and Natalie promptly tells the bride-to-be that "everyone thinks her fiancé is a crook." Oops.

Now, Anna is in a difficult position. Everyone is angry with her: Leah for not talking to her directly, Natalie for dragging her into things, and Leah's fiancé for making him look bad. Now what?

After a heated discussion, Anna knows she needs to step back and get her head clear. She knows that engaging after everyone is upset will only confuse things. Instead, she takes a journal and goes off for a moment by herself to think. Her head is swimming – is she in the wrong? Or is it all Natalie's fault for blabbing? How on earth can she make things right?

Consider the following "conversation" she writes in her journal, and see if you can identify the clarity questions, the possibility questions, and how these lead to insightful intention questions, which help her feel she has a solution going forward:

What am I feeling right now? Angry. Was only trying to help. Frustrated that Leah is in denial, and now I'm the bad guy even though I'm the one looking out for her. What am I thinking? I'm kicking myself. Should have just spoken to her directly. That was stupid. Natalie is such a gossip, I should have known. I guess I'm embarrassed... or guilty?

What is happening right now? Ok, zoom out. I've told the truth and now everyone's angry with me. No, that's not right. I've brought to everyone's attention an awkward issue right before a wedding. Would someone else agree with that assessment? Would Natalie or Leah?

I can tell I've activated a core belief here: this old thing of me needing to save everyone. Like I know best! But I've learnt from the past that I'm not responsible for other people. What is my role in this? Well, I talked to Natalie. That's my responsibility. But I didn't marry a complete loser who's lying about money!

Hang on a second. That makes me think: do I actually KNOW that any of this is true? And do I know that Leah is oblivious? I've just assumed she needs to be rescued, or told the "truth." When I write it out like I can see how arrogant that is... Maybe she feels I'm interfering and being insensitive. Maybe she knows and has chose, now I've made her uncomfortable. Wouldn't I feel attacked if I was her? Oops. Maybe I'm more in the wrong here than I thought.

Ok, If I do nothing here, I will alienate my friends. I need to say something. This situation could be cleared up. I could have more consideration for Leah. Could I talk to her directly and apologize? (oh, and Natalie too... I'll talk to her later, but I'm too upset right now).

I know what I value here: being honest, being a good friend, being a good person. I will apologize. I want to be the person who is big enough to know when they've overstepped. If I'm honest, a small part of me wanted to jeopardize her wedding (yikes! Is this a shadow thing? Hmm... that's something to think about).

I can't change how they feel now but I can change how I act right now.

I want to use my desire to help people wisely, and not allow myself to interfere or meddle. I'll talk directly with Leah, apologize, and say if she wants my help I'm always here for her. Then lay low for a while. There. Nothing more I can do for now. Lesson learnt.

Summary:

- Conversation is a powerful way to arrive at self-awareness, but we can also use questions in self-conversation to gain insight.
- Self-conversation is a way to gain greater objectivity and awareness.
- To avoid pointless rumination or navel-gazing, we can practice the art of using *what* questions instead of *why* questions. To use self-conversation to develop better awareness, we need to objectively use questions as tools of transformation, rather than allowing them to trap us in our perspectives.
- Three types of questions can help us increase internal and external self-awareness: the first is to gain **clarity** on the situation by asking *what is*. These

137

questions allow us to observe ourselves and the situation as it is, developing our internal self-awareness.

- The next is **possibility** questions, which expand our awareness by looking at what *could be*, and what opportunities exist within and without. This helps us become aware of our responsibility and scope for action.

- The final question type is **intention** questions, which bring awareness to our values and principles, our desires, and our agency in creating the life we want. Possibility and intention questions hone our external awareness and draw our attention to how they interact with our internal perception.

- We can use all three question types in journaling or literal out-loud dialogue with imaginary beings or versions of ourselves. The key is to generate insight that leads to action. A good question to ask is, *are my questions actually helping me?*

Chapter 5: Self-awareness is social awareness

And for most intents and purposes, social awareness is emotional intelligence. The best modern conception of emotional intelligence comes from psychologist Daniel Goleman.

Emotional intelligence is knowing and perceiving the emotions you feel and why you feel them, then transferring that type of awareness onto others. You are able to put a label on your emotional state and find its cause and effect. By extension, emotional intelligence is being able to read other people's emotions accurately and deduce the reasons for them.

When you start thinking "Why did she say that?" and "What made him do that?" instead of immediately reacting, that's the beginning of your path to emotional intelligence. It's a matter of understanding the whole causal chain of other people's motivations and intentions and how that leads to their emotions, which lead to their behaviors.

High emotional intelligence is like being able to read someone's mind. In reality, this everyday superpower is not so complex and requires resisting powerful aspects of human nature that behoove us to focus only on ourselves.

Take Charlotte. Charlotte prances into the office, her steps lilting and a smile on her face. Before sitting down, she asks her coworker a question: "What do you think of my new haircut?" Derek, her coworker, doesn't care what her hair looks like whatsoever, but he likes Charlotte, and he also knows that she often worries about her looks. "It looks great," he enthuses. "The new cut really brings out your eyes."

"I thought so too!" she gushes, taking her seat. "Thanks." She smiles.

Because Derek understood and cared about Charlotte's emotions, he knew she was asking for encouragement and praise rather than an apathetic dismissal. He read the situation and connected to her emotional state rather than to her simple and seemingly innocent question. His kind response bolstered her impression of his trustworthiness and kindness, raising her opinion of him.

Every time you improve your emotional intelligence, you'll have more interactions like these. It's about understanding and consideration and stepping outside of your own desires and perspectives. Daniel Goleman's modern conception of emotional intelligence can be described in four major categories. They all work together to create a blueprint for understanding and reading others more effectively.

Self-Awareness

When we're self-aware, we know who we are, what we think, and what we feel. We know that when we get depressed, we'll get less done. We know that when we drink coffee, we tend to be peppier and more productive. We understand that when we're feeling stressed, we're less likely to have patience for other people's needs. We recognize emotion as an underlying basis for most of our actions.

In short, we have knowledge of what we feel, why we feel that way, and how our feelings will impact our behavior. Self-aware people are also able to observe the effects their emotions have on other people. Happiness and sadness alike tend to be contagious, and a self-aware person will know that their emotions impact and are impacted by their environment.

Self-awareness also involves knowing our strengths and knowing weaknesses. More importantly, it helps us be willing and able to accept advice and criticism. People who aren't as aware of their real skills or value will either think they're too incompetent and incapable of learning or that they already know everything and don't need to be taught.

Neither is true of anyone, and people who fall into those traps come off as lazy or as arrogant know-it-alls, respectively. When you can admit you need help and accept the help or advice offered, you show other people that you value their opinion and respect their knowledge. Accepting help makes the people helping you feel important and needed, which is something we all appreciate. Stop thinking about your faults as bad things; they're really opportunities to make friends and learn new things.

You can improve your self-awareness in a lot of ways. Overall, you just need to know yourself better. Professional-level psychological or personality tests can give some insight, as can asking your friends to rate you on various personality traits or skills. It's also possible to watch how people respond to you when you do or say certain things and gain insight about what traits you have that contribute to their reactions.

Or you can simply sit and reflect upon things you've done and ask *why*. And then ask *why* again. And then do it three more times—this typically allows you to cut through the defenses you've constructed around yourself and get to the heart of matters. Anything that gives you feedback about why you feel your emotions is useful.

Take a step back and pause whenever you experience a strong emotion. Close your eyes and try to trace what happened in the past hour or two that led you to feel that way. Are there any facts or experiences in the past that would explain why you feel a particular way about certain things and people in your life? What is currently casting a subconscious shadow over your mood?

For example, if you're angry at 6:00 p.m., start thinking about what you've done since 3:00 p.m. You've driven home, had a snack, changed into your sweatpants, and watched a little bit of television.

When you visualize your drive home, though, suddenly you remember that you were cut off by somebody and that you were beeped at incessantly. This agitated you and you were still feeling the effects of that mood dampener hours later. This is a simplification of the process that begins to take place much more instantly.

The sad reality is that most people are not in tune with their feelings. Often, we are negatively affected by the emotional impact of things that have long since been irrelevant. Most people just react automatically without realizing why and without stopping to think what is happening internally. They fall into patterns that are sometimes negative and sometimes destructive.

Rather than looking inward and attempting to label your emotions based on what you might hypothesize caused them, you can also analyze how you are acting and label them that way. In the former, you are looking to the past to try to deduce a cause. In the latter, you are looking at the present to see the manifestation of emotion. In a sense, you are working backward from what you see and creating at least one theory about what caused it.

Just as with other people, you can tell more about yourself by your actions than you can by what you say (or what you tell yourself).

Self-Management

The most fundamental aspect of self-management is the ability to keep our emotions in check. When we're ecstatic because we got a date with a dreamboat, we don't let that excitement distract others in business meetings. When we're angry about being overlooked for a promotion, we don't let that impact our work relationship with our rival or our boss.

We even work to stay calm, steady, and effective when situations are stressful, hostile, or dangerous. In short, it involves not letting emotions get the best of you.

A lot of people attempt to do this by bottling up their emotions, but that's a bad idea because it can lead to resentment, bitterness, and even eventual explosions of hatred and rage. Our emotions help us understand what we really think about events and people. Paying attention to them can let us form rational descriptions of our concerns and joys that can let us impact our work and relationships in positive ways. Notice what you feel, examine why you feel it, and talk about it calmly with relevant parties when your head is clear. That will let you form meaningful compromises and help you gain more happiness in life. In short, express emotions in appropriate, productive ways; don't repress them. This step is the next step in being self-aware: what do you actually *do* with your emotions that you've identified?

Self-management also involves monitoring our thoughts and moods to manufacture a positive outlook. Some people are natural optimists, some aren't, but seeking out the opportunities and lessons in even the worst situations can produce a silver lining that allows for meaningful growth and progress. You can't let yourself be crushed by a failure; you have to push through it, learn everything it taught you by heart, and do better next time. A well-managed emotional life is used to motivate you toward your goals because you can use conscious patterns of optimistic thought to rally yourself with hope and joy, letting you continue on your journey. Everyone likes people who can encourage them to go on in the face of hardship, and developing this optimism will do exactly that.

The final trait in self-management is flexibility. A lot of people become attached to doing things a certain way and balk when a better method comes along. Others are so scared of change that they presume anything new must be bad. But a self-managed person will see those impulses as unhelpful and try to learn new ways of thinking and doing things. This helps them adapt and manage their expectations and emotions better.

Self-Motivation

Arguably a subset of self-management, self-motivation pushes people to meet and exceed expectations—because they know what emotions they want more and less of. They have a good guess on what will make them feel fulfilled, and they try to accomplish that constantly.

Self-motivated people continually look for ways to improve their emotional state. They know what makes them tick, emotionally and otherwise, and try to set themselves up for success. You can supercharge your ability to do this by noticing when you or others complain. Complaints indicate problems, which are opportunities for improvement. When you find these, think about ways to solve the problem, and when you can make those solutions happen, get to it!

Social Awareness

People who are socially aware can read the room and understand the emotions that groups and individuals are likely feeling.

At a group level, being socially aware means understanding the power structure and organization of groups, along with the emotional impact of those structures and the emotional currents that flow between one person and the next. It helps us interpret situations. Understanding that the secretary is happy to help her boss but is tired from overwork is part of social awareness.

It's also social awareness to know that she's more replaceable and therefore less important and that both she and her boss are influenced by that dynamic. It sounds like an overwhelming amount of data to process, but it can be simplified to asking why people have certain behaviors with one person versus another and then finding the dynamic that causes it.

Observing and interacting with people helps develop this skill. Whenever you see an interaction that puzzles or intrigues you, you can ask yourself why they're saying and doing what they are to try to get a better grasp of relationship dynamics. The better you get, the easier it will be to find the right things to do in social situations of every size and type. Obviously, this is a massive oversimplification, but it begins with asking why something is happening and what unseen or unconscious elements are causing it.

Ask yourself these questions, one at a time at first, and shortly they will become instinctual habit. It's not an easy task because you can't focus on one factor definitively. Each situation is different, and you must be adaptable in discovering why people feel what they do. Going through this checklist will assist you in reading people's emotions in a way you may never have considered before.

- How might your thoughts and actions be misinterpreted?
- What are other people's primary motivations and what unspoken, underlying motivations might they have that they (and you) are not even aware of?
- Consider people's built-in biases and life circumstances that give rise to certain emotions. What is their background and upbringing?
- How do people display their emotions both positively and negatively?
- How are emotions displayed in different ways?
- What emotions are they likely to be feeling and why?
- What is the purpose for what they are saying?
- What is their baseline emotional state

and preferred interaction style?

By being aware of these factors, you increase your emotional intelligence because you are able to read people more accurately. And just as important, you can respond to them in a more calibrated manner that leads to fewer negative reactions. Notably, this process can take a while—exactly the difference between responding and reacting.

At the most basic level, emotional intelligence is knowing the range of reactions to any given statement or circumstance and who might respond differently and why.

If you insult someone's mother in a serious manner and with a serious face, one reaction would be anger and being offended. You can expect that reaction a majority of the time. However, what are the other possible reactions, and what accounts for the difference? People might assume you are joking, laugh out of confusion, or ignore you because they didn't even hear what you said.

Emotional intelligence will allow you to connect with people on a deeper level because you understand them implicitly without their saying anything. You will just get them. This is what many people interpret as chemistry and rapport, and you will have it in a seemingly effortless manner.

You can see how emotional intelligence starts from yourself and then transfers to others. In the previous chapter, we focused a lot on values and deeper intentions, which inform how people would like to act. Here, we are paying more attention to emotions, which tells you how they will more naturally and instinctually act. Taken together, we are learning how to analyze someone's rational and emotional sides to both predict their behavior and also interpret it.

Social awareness and subtext

Communication is much more than the words that we speak or hear. Studies have quoted figures stating that 50% to 90% of communication—the message and emotion we get from others—is based on nonverbal or unspoken signals, starting from

Mehrabian and Ferris in "Inference of Attitudes from Nonverbal Communications in Two Channels" in 1967. Add that to additional communication based on subtext, context, implication, and inference, and you'll almost wonder what impact our actual words have.

Whatever the case, what we think we are communicating is often overshadowed or outright contradicted by what is meant to be interpreted between the lines. What we say is not really what we mean most of the time, and this is something we begin to learn as children. It's not that the words we use don't matter—they do. But the way in which we use them, and the contexts we use them in, are far more indicative of our feelings and emotions.

Unfortunately, for many of us, these small signs might as well be incantations for magic spells based on how subtle or convoluted they seem. One of the keys to communicating more clearly and being able to read between the lines of what people say is to understand *subtext*. To borrow from Chaney and Lyden's 1997 publication "Subtextual

Communication Impression Management: An Empirical Study," in the context of an office environment, subtext is the following:

> Subtextual communication, a covert language that strengthens or negates the spoken text, is used to influence the impressions other people have of us and may be used to competitive advantage in numerous situations in the workplace. The subtext is more subtle than the obvious text and may be more honest in interactions between people (Fast, 1991).

> Subtextual communication elements are related to image and may convey positive or negative impressions related to assurance, credibility, competence, and savoir-faire through dress, manner of introducing people, body language, regard for time, use of electronic communication, and dining etiquette.

Paul got a part-time job to give him extra cash as he got his university degree. He decided to work in a local electronics store because he knew the people, the area, and the product like the back of his hand. Imagine his surprise when he discovered he wasn't the big sales star he made himself out to be during the interview process.

Everyone else seemed to hit their sales quotas with ease, yet there he was, stuck barely reaching the lower end of the target. What made matters worse was the fact that other staff members had absolutely no technical knowledge, yet they surpassed Paul in sales every single month.

Paul's sales were so bad that his boss called him in for a performance meeting to address the problem. Instead of pointing out where Paul went wrong, he decided to match him up with his top salesman to discover how the sales techniques differed.

For the entire afternoon, Paul tagged along with the top-performing salesperson, Sam. As Paul observed, he noticed something interesting. The customers were all completely the same, the queries were all the same, and his solutions were the same—except for one small thing.

Where Paul would give up or move on, Sam offered additional recommendations and moved in for the kill. He realized this when a customer was looking at a camera. The customer raised his hands and declared the product to be "fine." At this point, Sam picked up a more expensive camera and walked the customer through its features. Paul wouldn't usually do that—when the customer said something was "fine," he would continue focusing on closing the sale on the same camera.

But to his surprise, the customer ended up buying the more expensive camera. As soon as the customer left the store, Paul asked Sam, "What made you suggest a whole new product? Isn't that just confusing the customer? I thought he said it was fine!"

Sam just laughed and said, "Just because the customer says it's fine doesn't mean it is. Fine is not positive. It usually means they want something more or their expectations haven't been met. It's them asking for more options in reality."

Paul was taking people's words literally and only at face value, and because of that, he was missing the real messages people were sending him. Whatever was being said was the only thing Paul was operating on, and he didn't consider that communication would occur in any other way. Sam explained that people's words were merely the tip of the iceberg in terms of what they wanted to communicate, and "fine" said with a flat speaking tone was as good as "this sucks." That one simple statement made a huge change in Paul's sales, as he began trying to dig beneath the words themselves and pick up on the meaning behind them.

Don't be like Paul. Learn subtext to read people better and begin to truly respond to what people are trying to communicate.

Communication can be divided into two categories: overt and covert. Overt is the words we say and the explicit messages we want to convey. This is when we directly tell someone that we're hungry and ask for a hamburger.

Subtext is the covert type of communication. It's almost never directly said, relies on literally anything besides the direct message coming out of someone's mouth, and requires correct interpretation. Using subtext to say "I'm hungry" would include rubbing your stomach, licking your lips, pointing out that there is a menu on a nearby table, and mentioning that your previous meal was tiny.

Not everyone is going to pick up on those signs, but it is undeniable what the person wanted to convey. We routinely communicate through these indirect means and hope that it saves us the trouble of being direct. Subsequently, understanding the subtext under and surrounding people's seemingly benign statements gives you insight into their true feelings and thoughts.

For example, how does the overt dialogue below differ from the subtextual, covert message? Here, it's what is *not said* that completes the message. The subtext is that the question wasn't replied to in a convincing manner and, thus, is less than sincere. Suppose the answerer of the question has a history of being blunt.

"Am I fat?"
"No, you're not fat."
Translation: Yes, you might be a little bit fat.

"Am I fat?"
"No, but I suppose you could maybe lose a couple of pounds."
Translation: Yeah, you're definitely fat now.

Subtext can be delivered through vocal tone, phrasing, delivery, reference to prior experiences, knowledge of relationships, body language, gesticulation, circumstances, and even moods. It sounds abstract and confusing, but just imagine that subtext is everything we want to say besides the *exact words* we use.

In fact, that's one of the big reasons we use it. It allows us to navigate the world through indirect and nonconfrontational means. If you're great at subtext, it saves time, it's efficient, and it imparts great emotional intelligence by understanding people's ever-shifting circumstances.

Subtext appears in every situation, from work and dating to social situations and family dynamics. In fact, much of dating can be said to be subtext because much of sexual tension depends on not revealing true intentions up front. If you ask someone to dinner and they tell you they are busy, they might be busy, or they might not be interested. If you ask the same person out four times and each time they say they're busy, then there is additional subtext for you to read. Take the context into account and things aren't looking good for you on the romantic front.

Through our behavior and choice of words, we transmit clues and desperately hope people pick up on them. Of course, this is the origin of passive-aggressive behavior—we don't feel comfortable saying something directly, so our indirect measures become more and more aggressive and unpleasant. As a species, we are fairly avoidant and nonconfrontational. Not many people feel comfortable wearing their opinions and hearts on their sleeves, especially when they clash with those of other people. Directness is inherently tense, so it's something we prefer to avoid.

A helpful method to imagine how subtext works in social situations is to imagine how it factors into a novel or a screenplay. When you're watching a movie or reading a book, you don't usually get told what the characters understand, feel, or think, and despite that, you come away with a clear sense of meaning about the scenes and relationships. This is all because of subtext.

In this context, it's commonly referred to as what is *under the skin of the character*— what drives and motivates them, what they feel toward everyone else in the story, and what's under the surface of all of their actions. Without giving characters clear motivations and having everyone in the movie operate only on a "what you see is what you get" level, you end up with a flat movie with no emotional impact.

Even in movies, there can be ambiguity in the subtext—sometimes intentional and sometimes not. This is the part the audience must fill in, which is why two people can come out of a film and have radically different ideas about the meaning the director was trying to convey.

Let's take a look at an example scene in detail to illustrate this clearly. Always remember that we have to separate the covert and overt communication.

Imagine a room where a man clasps a tiny baby-blue box in his hands. The table is decorated with roses and Champagne. A woman appears at the side of the frame and prepares to leave the room. She does not notice the man in the corner. He says, "Wait!"

Why does the man call the woman?

If you say, "Because he wants to propose to her," you have understood the subtext present in this basic scene. The dialogue never says that the man wants to propose marriage to the woman. You inferred that from a combination of the mood, the description, and the scene itself.

Is the word "wait" subtext? In this scene, the man is telling the woman to stop. There is nothing hidden in his words other than "Don't go!" or perhaps "Stay!" depending on how the word is delivered.

Imagine instead that the man overtly says, "I have a table laid out here for you and I intend to propose with this beautiful ring I bought from Tiffany & Co." It's not something that would happen in real life, and thus, movies have to be written with subtext that allows people to understand what's happening.

Filling in the details of any incoming communication through subtext is integral to better communication and greater likability. If you look closely, you will soon find that almost everything a person says has shades of subtext meant to consciously or unconsciously communicate additional messages.

Pay attention to people's prior history and experiences and how they might relate to the current situation. What emotions are at play here? Hint: there is always at least one primary emotion at play. It will inevitably color their perspectives, priorities, and motivations in a way that could make their message differ from their words. If you know someone's general personality traits, you can often make a call by analyzing the situation from how they would prefer to conduct themselves. If someone is extremely meek and quiet and says something to the effect of "I agree... I suppose," then it probably means they are internally screaming "NO!" Essentially, consider the source and how a person's experiences color their communication.

Judge someone's authenticity by analyzing the tone of their voice. Are they angry, serious, or sarcastic? Does the tone match the message? If someone says yes but they use a sarcastic tone, then they probably mean no. If someone says yes but they are angry, then they are probably not happy with the outcome. If they are serious and they say yes, then they are conflicted or they probably don't care. There is a virtually unlimited number of interpretations of vocal tone, but most of them indeed mean that the words aren't meant to be taken at face value.

Observe how people respond to you. When you look at how patient people are, how nice they act, and how accommodating they try to be, you can gauge how they feel about what you say. This also extends to how much silence you hear and how much interest they show. If someone takes two beats to answer a simple question, they had to think about their reply and may be using subtext to communicate negativity even if they agree with you.

Another aspect to consider, which may require more intense observational skills, is to see how much they deviate from their usual pattern of behavior. If your supervisor is typically upbeat, what does it mean that they are somber and negative? It can turn a proclamation of "Things are going well..." into the exact opposite message.

Subtext leaves clues that you can harness to become an expert communicator. People leave signs everywhere.

Of course, the tough part is deciphering these aspects of people simultaneously and instantly, as you might do in a normal everyday conversation. This means you actually have two tasks: (1) processing the conversation and responding appropriately and (2) being on the lookout for subtextual cues. You might be able to train yourself to pick up on specific types of subtext and social cues, but can you pick up on them while trying to find others? Or will you only be able to observe so many things at once? It might seem like you'd need three brains and six pairs of eyes to pick up on so many things at once—at the beginning, this might be true.

But the only thing we can do is start small and train yourself until these things become a subconscious habit to consider—*why did they say that, what are they feeling, and what could it mean?*

I want to end the section on subtext with a small exercise to get you into the mood. It's fairly easy: go out into public and observe people interacting—for example, sitting at a café and covertly watching the people at nearby tables. You can't hear the overt conversation, so you're going to make a guess at the subtext of the covert communication. Assign backstories, emotions, and motivations to the people you are observing. Go out on a limb and make up stories. Once you get better at subtext, you'll find that the stories you create in situations like this will become more and more accurate.

Social awareness and intelligence

We began this book with a consideration of how the skills of self-awareness and social awareness were almost like two sides of the same coin – develop one and you can't help but develop the other. Emotionally intelligent people invariably are socially intelligent people. There is a lively and dynamic relationship between themselves, their environment and others. They can go within and understand themselves, but they're also able to communicate that self to others, and hear about perspectives that are not theirs. They can take their insights and not only use them to cooperate with others, but allow themselves to change and evolve. It's a constant flow back and forth – a meta-conversation between self and other.

We began with a few chapters on understanding our own level of self-awareness, our personal obstacles and blind spots to better awareness, and how to use self-conversation to improve. The next step is obvious: we take what we learn and externalize it.

Social intelligence is easy to define: it's simply the capacity to properly manage the social landscape you find yourself in. If you've ever known someone who was enormously intelligent yet didn't exactly succeed in life because they were socially awkward, you already know that social intelligence is a big part of effectively navigating life.

Strong, beneficial, mature relationships keep us physically healthy, they keep us mentally healthy, and they help us stay grounded in empathy and consideration for others. Collaboration and harmony are not just nice ideas – they are a minimum requirement for success in a complex, difficult world. The quality of our relationships directly affects our careers and financial life, our family life, our identities, our resilience, our sense of belonging and purpose – everything.

If you're not that socially intelligent, don't worry. After all, this is a skill that can be learnt, and the first major step is to know what capacities you're lacking. Here are a few things to remember.

Think about the bigger picture

We're often encouraged to think about socializing and conversations as purely verbal phenomena. But the words we use are just the tip of the iceberg. Realize that when you communicate to the outside world, you do so with your *entire self*:

Your words, and the content of your speech
Your macro- and micro-expressions
Your voice – its pitch, tone, volume, accent
Your breath
The gestures you make
Your reactions to others
Your posture and the way you hold yourself
Your overall attitude and emotional expression
Your manner of dress and presentation
How much of the available time or space you're taking up
Your physicality (your body is sending chemical messages all the time broadcasting your age, sex, state of health etc.)

Social intelligence comes down to being an aware and proactive communicator. It means understanding the meta-language that people use, and knowing how yours is affecting others. You cannot be socially switched on unless you possess enough **awareness** – of self and others. To get better at this, you need only practice.

Friendly, cooperative encounters are typically characterized by openness and warmth. Think of all the millions of ways you can communicate these two ideas!

Whenever you can remember, try to notice the quality of interactions you have with others. Those that feel good – why? What made you like person A but feel weird around person B? Pay attention to all the little pieces of data being transmitted whenever two people get together.

At first, you might like to just "people watch" from a distance. In your conversations, it's a good idea to sometimes ignore the words people are saying and read everything else. What are they feeling? Thinking? What are their intentions? Are they communicating tension or relaxation? Are they advancing or retreating? Warm or cold?

Get in sync
Think of two people dancing salsa. They need to be hearing the same music, dancing on the same beat. They need to be following one another, tuned into the other one's style, listening closely so they can move together as one. Social interaction is the same. Accurate perception is a big piece of the puzzle, but so is *attunement*. There needs to be smooth, synchronous interaction.

How do you create this feeling of being in sync? Conversations and social interactions are living, breathing things. They're spontaneous and emergent, so we need to be alert, receptive and responsive in the moment if we want to create seamless interactions. Have you ever tried turning up to a conversation with a memorized script of what you wanted to say? You probably noticed how the actual conversation did its own thing anyway. That's because you are not solely in charge of it – you are *mutually creating* it with the other person. So, anything can happen. And good interactions are those where people respect this fact.

Assumptions and judgment kill an interaction. Curiosity and open-mindedness keep it alive. Remind yourself constantly about the ultimate goal of conversations: mostly, it's either about enjoyment or the transmission of information. Or both. If you see a conversation as just a battleground or a place to show off, you're doing it wrong! The fortification of the ego is not the purpose, but connection and flow with the other person are what matters.

Try as hard as you can to stay curious. One clever way to do this is to examine any statements or foregone conclusions you have internally and transform these into questions. Don't think, "he's only 12, he knows nothing about life" but, "I wonder what he knows that I don't?" Instead of just relying on stereotypes or labels, *really look* at the person in front of you. Just observe without value judgment. Instead of stale, boring conclusions that go nowhere, be willing to be surprised by how interesting people can be.

Another good trick is to reflect. Notice how the other person is communicating, and match that, either by mirroring their body language, paraphrasing their statements or copying their facial expression. This sends a very primal message: *I'm here, I'm paying attention, I'm friendly, and I'm attempting to synchronize with you.* That leads us neatly to...

Be more empathetic

When we have low self-awareness, we can ironically spend a lot of time thinking about ourselves, becoming self-absorbed and forgetting about the other people in our world. It sounds too obvious to be true, but many of us falsely assume that everyone else in a situation shares the same emotional interpretation of events, that they are paying attention to the same things we are, or that they value different aspects the same way we do.

The basis of empathy is imagination – we need to imagine a world different from our own. And to do this, we need enough imagination to realize there even *is* an emotional perspective besides our own! Without empathy, we cannot synchronize or attune to others, but instead, get trapped in our own tunnel vision.

Empathy is not some magical trait that only a chosen few are blessed with. Empathy is not a characteristic but an act – and any person can show empathy. We'll look at empathy in more detail in the next section, but as you interact with people, try to learn of the fact that they are inhabiting an emotional world just as rich and nuanced as your own – and which might not only be different but also make little sense to you!

Use the wheel of emotions to help you identify what they may be feeling. Ask questions – a lot! Squeeze in mini-validations that show your understanding, like "oh that makes sense" or "I get you!" Something you might not have thought of is reading the "energy" or feeling of the whole room or situation in general. People synchronize and attune to one another in bigger groups, too. What's the vibe of the gathering? What are the unspoken rules? What role are you expected to play here? Getting on the same frequency in this way is a big part of social awareness.

Know your triggers
Often, we react poorly in social situations or fail to find the "flow" because we've been triggered into old memories or core beliefs that hinder us from connecting. Goleman explains two processing modes: the first he calls the Low Road, which refers to the knee-jerk, immediate instinctual reactions heavy on emotion. They're gut feelings and they're

based on split-second, primal and unconscious perceptions. The High Road is our slower but more rational mind, and it helps us proactively communicate, analyze, and understand the world.

When triggered by things that cause us to go into our automatic beliefs, when we are unaware and reactive, then we are on the Low Road, and might not be communicating and we could. For example, someone saying goodbye at the end of a visit may trigger very old abandonment issues and fearful core beliefs that stem from your childhood. If you react to this trigger, however, you are no longer in the flow of the moment.

You can make incredible progress with your own shadow, your unconscious core beliefs and your hidden hang-ups by carefully examining what social situations trigger you. What makes you most anxious? Be curious about what is setting you off. Usually, it's not the situation itself but your interpretation of it.

When you know the baggage you bring to any interaction, you can make more informed choices and connect more authentically to the people around you.

You'll be able to accurately tell what portion of every interaction is truly *yours*, and what is the other person's. You won't be blaming others unfairly, nor you will be accepting any blame you shouldn't – in other words, knowing your triggers allows you to set up clearer and healthier boundaries. In our example above, you can tell that the person isn't literally abandoning you, and so you need not get in conflict or misunderstanding with them.

Be an active listener
Being a good listener is a lot like being self-aware – everyone *thinks* they are, but few are correct! Be honest: do you enter conversations mainly to be heard? Do you judge the success of an interaction according to how well the other person understands, agrees with or approves of you? Being seen and validated is such a fundamental human need that we can all be forgiven for forgetting the other side of things: that we also need to listen.

Active listening does *not* mean being passive or doing nothing. It's not about waiting for the other person to stop talking so you can get a "turn." Rather, listening is a focused and skillful perception of the other person.

Here's the good news – if you've practiced being aware and receptive with yourself, you'll be much more able to do it with others. Let go of biases, assumptions, expectations, and all the nonsense your ego comes up with, and simply observe what is in front of you. Be charitable and assume that the person in front of you is generally good, that they have something to teach you, and that their perspective is no more or less valid than your own.

Being a good listener is so much more than politely saying "uh huh" as the other person talks. It's about bestowing your full and uncompromised attention on the other person. Really see them. Try to immerse in their world and grasp what they're communicating – on all channels, and in all ways. Listening in this way is a profound act of kindness and empathy. Just listening acts to validate someone, telling them that their perspective, their expression and their whole selves are worth paying attention to. In a world where, arguably, everyone is starving for attention, this can be an incredibly fast way of connecting with people.

Here's a trick to instantly be a better listener: the next time you're in a conversation and find yourself thinking of something you want to say, stop yourself and instead ask the other person a question. Think of it like hitting the tennis ball right back to their side of the court. Experiment with not being in the limelight – can you find enjoyment in letting someone else shine?

Another great trick is to make sure that when you do speak, do so only after a pause. We may rush in to speak if we're excited, or even interrupt the other person, but when you pause for a moment and let their words sink in, you show you value their perspective and are not just there to listen to your voice. Slow down and relax. Paraphrase what you've heard or ask questions that encourage them to carry on speaking. Treat your conversation partner like they're the most fascinating person on the planet, and you'll both soon be in that flow.

Training empathy
Lesson 1: understand what empathy is
Imagine somebody says, "I'm depressed."

Their psychiatrist says, "Yes, I understand. I'm the country's leading expert on depression and I know exactly what you're going through. After all, I wrote the book on this kind of depression!"

Their mother says, "When you're miserable, I'm miserable! I haven't slept a wink since you told me you're depressed."

Their friend says, "I can't imagine how hard it must feel right now. Want to come over tonight and we get some pizza and talk it over?"

Which one is empathy? Well, they all are. There are (at least) three types of empathy, and to be as socially aware as possible, we need to learn the difference. Every experience we have has different components – the physical, the cognitive, the emotional. It follows then that we can have empathy on these different channels, too. Empathizing is entering into someone else's experience. We can do this in 3 ways:

Cognitive empathy is intellectually understanding and grasping another's perspective – like the psychiatrist above. You can perfectly comprehend another person's position, but you don't feel what they feel. This can be extremely useful when negotiating, in diplomacy or problem solving, as it allows an expanded perspective that isn't compromised by strong emotions. But cognitive empathy is precisely what abusers might use when they want to understand what will best hurt or deceive their victims!

Emotional empathy is the most common type. It's "feeling with" someone, literally as though their emotions were also yours. This is the mother's reaction. It's genuine, it comes from a good place, but as you can see, it's not always useful – in this case, there are now two depressed people instead of one! Emotional empathy is human and natural. It allows us to care, respond to others, and take responsibility. However, "emotional contagion" is not all that useful. If you have poor boundaries, and get enmeshed or overwhelmed by other people's emotions, you lose your ability to self-regulate – plus, you can't help them out of their distress.

Compassionate empathy is almost like empathy in action. We feel someone's suffering, but we remain objective enough to help them make a move towards ending that suffering. We take action, or help them take action, to solve the problem. Getting alongside someone to concretely improve their lives is arguably the most practical form of empathy you can show them. There's a dark side to this too – we have to be careful not to interfere, meddle or make assumptions about what we think is best for others.

This leads us to the next obvious point: *all three* types of empathy are necessary for healthy and happy relationships. Ideally, we'd be able to intellectually understand someone's problem and feel some of what they're feeling. We'd also be objective enough to help them do something about it. You don't want to go to a doctor who acts like a logic robot, but you also don't want a doctor who themselves will burst into tears when telling you your diagnosis!

Too much cognitive empathy can be felt as cold or under-involved, while too much emotional empathy is smothering and over-involved. Compassionate empathy (i.e. the one with more objectivity!) helps you find the balance. This is the friend's response. They show concern and sympathy, but they lead with a kind gesture that may improve the situation.

How do we practically use these three empathy types in our daily lives? It's best to go sequentially: start by letting the other person know you understand intellectually. Then express sympathy so they know that you feel what they do, too. Finally, put your empathy to use and do something to help. This need not be advice, by the way. You can help someone enormously by making simple observations or suggestions, offering help, or pointing them toward something they need. But remember, it's about what *they* need – not what you need or what you think they need.

Lesson 2: look for what unites, not what divides

We all have prejudices. We all make assumptions and label people, reducing their complex and multifaceted selves down to stereotypes. But the truth is, we have a lot more in common with one another than it looks on the surface. To have empathy, we need to actively resist focusing on our differences, and instead, look for commonalities.

And it's not just outright hatred and preconceptions that keep us from compassion – any time we make lazy assumptions about people or craft pet theories about who they are without actually talking to them, we are robbing ourselves of the opportunity to know what they're like. Empathetic people give others the benefit of the doubt. If they can't immediately discern any similarities, they assume they just haven't discovered them yet. At the very least, every person you encounter is a human, who has loved and lost, with hopes and dreams and fears, and who was once an innocent child. When you respect other people in this way, you may be surprised to find your sense of dignity and self-esteem increasing!

In any conversation, try to focus on what is shared. In what ways are you aligned? What is similar? What can you agree on? It may help, especially in conflicts, to literally say, "I'm on your side!" or "let's find the middle ground." Often, people only appear to disagree on the surface. When you get down to it, most people are similar: they love their families, they want to do the right thing, and they're happy to compromise if they feel they're being heard and respected.

Speak to the best in everyone and assume that they're doing their best; the fastest way to alienate someone is to engage with them as though they're your enemy. Remember that it is always possible to say, "we disagree and can't find common ground, but I still respect you and I'm still listening." You can always demonstrate that you value the relationship, even if you don't agree with their perspective.

Lesson 3: understand theory of mind
Without getting too bogged down in the philosophy, what is going on in another person's mind? We only know our minds (if we're lucky!) but what is it like to be somebody else? We can never really know – but we can guess. This is what theory of mind boils down to – the theory we make for ourselves of another being's mind. This is the ability to see that other people are out there and that their experience is necessarily different from ours. It's the root of empathy, and it's not automatic; young children gradually develop the awareness that they are minds living in a world of other minds, and those other minds have intentions, emotions, thoughts – and even theories about them!

We may be laughing at the movie we're watching, but looking over at our friend, we

185

see them cringing and we can ascribe another emotion – an emotion we don't share – to their experience. We can comprehend that their opinion and perspective are different to ours. Understanding that their experience is as valid to them as ours is to us, is the start of genuine empathy. We can say, "she probably hates this movie because the jokes are hitting a bit close to home, given her background... maybe we should watch something different."

Everything everyone does comes from their unique collection of past experiences, mental models, habits, upbringing, culture and more. If you are having trouble empathizing with someone, pause and think of yourself for a second. Think of how large, complete and valid your own experience feels to you. Think of how everything *fits*, and how all your ideas are natural extensions and consequences of where you're coming from. In other words, you make sense! Now, turn your attention to the other person. Try to see that, in the same way, they make sense, too. If you cannot quite perceive that, it doesn't mean there is something wrong with their perspective, but there is an obstacle to your accessing it.

Often, this obstacle is the desire to center ourselves. Completely unconsciously, we may assume that we are at the center of the universe, that our perspective is more right, more obvious, more real, more accurate or even more moral than other people's. But it isn't. And if we conduct ourselves as though it were, we will never truly engage with others, but always compete, argue or ignore their perspectives. This is a loss for them and a loss for us.

One easy way to stop the habit of automatically centering yourself is to force yourself to regularly consider someone else's perspective. Think of someone you know well. Imagine they have a reality filter made up of all their beliefs, experiences and idiosyncrasies. Think of this filter as an abstract version of that person in your brain. Now ask yourself, "what would this person think or feel?"

You can never truly occupy another person's mind, but by "trying on" different perspectives this way, you can expand your own and welcome fresh insights. Your perspective has limits. Sometimes we *think* we are being empathetic when we say, "How would I feel if I were in their shoes?" We pass their experience through our own filter. But you go one level deeper when you can say, "How do *they* feel to be in their shoes?" You are acknowledging not just their experience but the filter they are using to process it. Big difference. "I personally think this movie is hilarious, but I can see from her point of view that it must look pretty offensive."

Lesson 4: use your imagination

Empathy is an exercise in imagination. We could stay trapped in our own direct experience forever, never looking outside our perceptions and encountering nothing beyond them. But when we imagine that there's something – *someone* – else out there, the whole world opens up.

This opening up makes you more empathetic, yes. But, at the same time, it broadens and enriches your own life. We all operate from within our worldviews. We may not even realize the interpretations we're putting on reality, our assumptions, the values we assign events, or how we selectively focus on some things and ignore others. We can gain significant insights, however, when we entertain the possibility there is another approach or perspective available to us. Thus, empathy can be used not just to understand someone else's viewpoint, but also to shed fresh light on our own.

Naturally empathetic people are in the habit of constantly realizing they are using a filter in the first place. They are comfortable being aware of and even questioning their knee-jerk perceptions. We encountered this earlier as "objectivity" – the ability to step back from your experience and ask, "I wonder if this could be some other way?"

One excellent way to strengthen this ability is to read. Changing language is a powerful way to shift perspectives because so much of our filter *is* language – our personal myths and narratives, our filter itself, is made of thoughts, labels, and impressions primarily verbal. So, when we immerse ourselves in someone else's linguistic world (i.e. in a book), we are getting a glimpse of their perspective on reality. We see *firsthand* their interpretation, their value-judgments, their focus and their intention. This differs from merely staying within our perspective and imagining theirs from afar.

To be better at empathy, read as often as possible. Choose literary fiction that varies in style and tone. Seek authors from different backgrounds and historical periods. It's not deciding whether you agree or not, whether you like it, or to what extent you are similar. You are merely exercising your empathy muscle by exploring differences. Fiction can help you translate cognitive empathy into emotional empathy. Books are a powerful technology – they are theory of mind machines!

Summary:

- Better understanding people's emotions begins with understanding your own. This comes in the form of emotional intelligence, and Daniel Goleman's conception of emotional intelligence consists of self-awareness (what do I feel and why), self-management (how can I express my emotions safely and learn from them), self-motivation (what makes me happy, and how can I achieve that), and social awareness (what are other people feeling and why. The whole process begins with understanding yourself and then realizing that everyone else has the same amount of unconscious and hidden thoughts that dictate their emotions and actions. It is a way of thinking that must be trained and allows you to pull a significant amount of information from a small interaction.

- Likewise, we must learn to understand subtextual cues better. This is related to the social awareness element of emotional intelligence. We must realize that most communication is covert, and yet most of us are only responding to communication that is overt. This means we frequently miss the true meaning of people's words and actions. The easiest way to adopt this particular method of thinking is to ask, *why did they say that, what are they feeling, and what could it mean?*

- With greater self-awareness, we become able to perceive and engage more accurately with others, and develop better social awareness. Daniel Goleman's concept of emotional intelligence shows us this capacity to communicate, empathize and engage with others is a separate and fundamental skill for success in life.

- To develop our social awareness, we need to expand our own inner perceptions outward. We can do this by being conscious of how we all communicate with others, including nonverbal communication such as body language and pitch of voice.
- Social awareness rests on synchronizing with others socially. We can do this by mirroring and reflecting to show we are attuned with others – this takes awareness. A great way to do this is with active listening: don't interrupt or center yourself, but give the other person time to shine.
- You can increase social awareness by acknowledging and taking responsibility for your own triggers, hang ups and baggage. This means you encounter others freely in the moment.
- Training empathy improves communication and social interactions. Empathy is the ability to step into the experience of someone else, and it can be developed in many ways. First, discern between the different types: cognitive, emotional or compassionate. It's best to offer people a blend of all three.

- Consistently try to look for what is common between you and the people you engage with, instead of focusing on difference. Assume people are fundamentally good and doing their best.
- Theory of mind refers to the guesses we make about someone else's inner experience. We improve empathy when we understand that people have different perspectives, feelings, thoughts and identities than we do.
- Finally, since empathy can be thought of as an exercise in imagination, we can become more empathetic by reading literary fiction and deeply exploring other worldviews.

Summary Guide

CHAPTER 1: THE THREE LEVELS OF SELF-AWARENESS

- There are two types of self-awareness: *internal* (how aware we are of our thoughts, feelings and identities) and *external* (how aware we are of how we are perceived by others). Internal awareness doesn't always imply external awareness. We can be seekers (low on both types), introspectors (high only on internal SA), people-pleasers (high only on external SA) or fully aware (high on both).

- Self-awareness develops as a capacity throughout life, and progresses through stages. Level 1 concerns the awareness of what you are doing and the causes of behavior. Level 2 is about awareness of what you are feeling, which is often concealed by what you are doing. Level 3 is awareness not only of thoughts, feelings and actions, but of what is being pushed out of awareness or avoided. This is the stage of deeper insight into the self.

- Kegan's theory of adult development showed that self-awareness matures with age, with people gradually acquiring more objectivity. We can progress through stages, where we **transform** (that is, change the way we perceive, rather than the content of what we perceive) and make **subject-object shifts**.

- We mature when we transform from subjective experience to objective. This can be simplified as the ability to see you "**have**" a quality that you can step back from and observe, rather than you "**are**" a quality that you are completely identified with.

- We can see increasing self-awareness as a project of gaining more objectivity in place of subjective identification.

CHAPTER 2: REASSESSING BELIEFS FROM YOUR PAST, AND YOUR DARK SIDE

- We can improve self-awareness by becoming conscious of our ingrained core beliefs that come from childhood. By understanding the "program" we run, we can make changes and live with more purpose and deliberation.
- We can ask where we first experienced an emotion, and what core beliefs this instilled in us in the past. We can then examine this core belief and look at the effect it has on our lives. Finally, we can ask if we would like to change this belief into something that better helps us create the life we want for ourselves.
- We are often driven by aspects of ourselves that we have pushed out of conscious awareness, i.e. what Jung called the shadow. We heal when we consciously integrate this material, with awareness and acceptance. We know the shadow is at work when we feel unclear about why we act, have disproportionate responses to events, or project onto others.
- There are many simple ways to integrate the shadow, become aware of core beliefs and gently rewrite them. They all rely on awareness.

- We can become aware of what we are most triggered by, and examine who we judge most, to see if we're projecting. We can practice meditation and mindfulness to increase objectivity. By noticing what emotions we feel resistant to, we can practice bearing and accepting them.
- We can also closely examine our cognitive biases and the core beliefs we've picked up during our lives. This goes hand in hand with learning to name and own emotions. Emotional literacy is a way to improve self-awareness and help us get distance from our immediate experience.

CHAPTER 3: FIND YOUR VALUES, BIG AND SMALL

- A value is a rule, principle, or belief that gives meaning to your life. It is usually something you consider very important in life and base many of your decisions around. This is why when you're confused about what to do in a certain situation or circumstances that you find yourself in, the cause is usually a lack of clarity on what your real values are.

- If you're not sure what your values are in life, don't worry; discovering them is not hard. However, the process does take time, and you won't simply wake up tomorrow with complete knowledge of what your values are.
- The first step to discovering what your values are is to simply abandon all preconceived notions you have of who you are. Often, the values we have been living by are actually derived externally. This can be through our family, culture, historical era, etc. By starting from a clean slate, we avoid such influences from clouding our judgment regarding our true values.
- Next, think about the things that you feel most strongly about. This could be personal success, close family bonds, serving others in the form of social work, etc. Finding one will often lead you to other values you hold because they point to a "higher" value you possess. Thus, valuing family over career means that your interpersonal relationships in general are valuable to you.
- Once you have a complete list of values, think about your goals in life and how your values align with them. Are the

things you're doing now in conjunction with your values and goals? If not, think of ways you can change that and live a life that is truer to your real self.

- As you discover your values, doing actions that promote them will help you decide what it is that you really consider important.

CHAPTER 4: WE DON'T TALK ANYMORE!

- Conversation is a powerful way to arrive at self-awareness, but we can also use questions in self-conversation to gain insight.
- Self-conversation is a way to gain greater objectivity and awareness.
- To avoid pointless rumination or navel-gazing, we can practice the art of using *what* questions instead of *why* questions. To use self-conversation to develop better awareness, we need to objectively use questions as tools of transformation, rather than allowing them to trap us in our perspectives.
- Three types of questions can help us increase internal and external self-

awareness: the first is to gain **clarity** on the situation by asking *what is*. These questions allow us to observe ourselves and the situation as it is, developing our internal self-awareness.

- The next is **possibility** questions, which expand our awareness by looking at what *could be*, and what opportunities exist within and without. This helps us become aware of our responsibility and scope for action.

- The final question type is **intention** questions, which bring awareness to our values and principles, our desires, and our agency in creating the life we want. Possibility and intention questions hone our external awareness and draw our attention to how they interact with our internal perception.

- We can use all three question types in journaling or literal out-loud dialogue with imaginary beings or versions of ourselves. The key is to generate insight that leads to action. A good question to ask is, *are my questions actually helping me?*

CHAPTER 5: SELF-AWARENESS IS SOCIAL AWARENESS

- Better understanding people's emotions begins with understanding your own. This comes in the form of emotional intelligence, and Daniel Goleman's conception of emotional intelligence consists of self-awareness (what do I feel and why), self-management (how can I express my emotions safely and learn from them), self-motivation (what makes me happy, and how can I achieve that), and social awareness (what are other people feeling and why. The whole process begins with understanding yourself and then realizing that everyone else has the same amount of unconscious and hidden thoughts that dictate their emotions and actions. It is a way of thinking that must be trained and allows you to pull a significant amount of information from a small interaction.
- Likewise, we must learn to understand subtextual cues better. This is related to the social awareness element of emotional intelligence. We must realize that most communication is covert, and yet most of us are only responding to communication that is overt. This means

we frequently miss the true meaning of people's words and actions. The easiest way to adopt this particular method of thinking is to ask, *why did they say that, what are they feeling, and what could it mean?*

- With greater self-awareness, we become able to perceive and engage more accurately with others, and develop better social awareness. Daniel Goleman's concept of emotional intelligence shows us this capacity to communicate, empathize and engage with others is a separate and fundamental skill for success in life.

- To develop our social awareness, we need to expand our own inner perceptions outward. We can do this by being conscious of how we all communicate with others, including nonverbal communication such as body language and pitch of voice.

- Social awareness rests on synchronizing with others socially. We can do this by mirroring and reflecting to show we are attuned with others – this takes awareness. A great way to do this is with active listening: don't interrupt or center yourself, but give the other person time to shine.

- You can increase social awareness by acknowledging and taking responsibility for your own triggers, hang ups and baggage. This means you encounter others freely in the moment.

- Training empathy improves communication and social interactions. Empathy is the ability to step into the experience of someone else, and it can be developed in many ways. First, discern between the different types: cognitive, emotional or compassionate. It's best to offer people a blend of all three.

- Consistently try to look for what is common between you and the people you engage with, instead of focusing on difference. Assume people are fundamentally good and doing their best.

- Theory of mind refers to the guesses we make about someone else's inner experience. We improve empathy when we understand that people have different perspectives, feelings, thoughts and identities than we do.

- Finally, since empathy can be thought of as an exercise in imagination, we can become more empathetic by reading literary fiction and deeply exploring other worldviews.